RV TWEAKS MODIFICATIONS and UPGRADES Volume II

By James Edward Clicquennoi

Text Copyright 2017 James Edward Clicquennoi

ISBN 9781792191299

Dedicated to My Wife who has put up with my RV hobby for the past thirty three years and supported me when I made the huge leap into a motorhome.

Dedicated to my grandchildren who ask "Grampa when are we going camping again"?

My thanks to Tom Geiss for his assistance with the cover collage.

Read my other books

"Motorhome Maintenance DIY and Save"

"My Best RV DIY Projects"

available at www.Amazon.com.

Traveling with my parents when younger and then my own family I have been RVing for over 60 years. Between my father and I we have owned 9 different types of RVs from simple pop ups, travel trailers, and finally a diesel pusher motorhome. In that time we have never taken our RV to anyone else for repairs or to add modifications. In my later life not only have I done all my own repairs but I have helped friends and colleagues in my travel clubs do theirs. In the past 15 years I began enhancing my RVs as well as friends with those options not installed by the manufacturer. This book describes with pictures and illustrations the close to 100 modifications I have performed. Some are simple and inexpensive while others are very complex. In installing these modifications my goal has been to make them all appear as original equipment fitted to the RV by the manufacturer.

The book is laid out to so that you can read the entire text front to back or more appropriately select one section and read what is required to perform that modification. I have included parts lists and links where material can be found that are all current as of the writing. In the event a link no longer functions most of the parts can be found by searching for the item name on the internet.

Table of Contents

I thought I would begin with a little background. Some of my earliest camping memories are with my parents and brother in our 1959 Shasta travel trailer. Back then it was state of the art. Looking back I wonder how we survived, no bathroom, no furnace, a ten gallon water tank with a hand pump, and one of the smallest propane refrigerators you have ever seen. The Shasta slept six and my position was on the back canvas bunk over the main bed. That bunk was so small that not only could I not sit up but I could not even roll over without hitting the ceiling. My dad pulled the Shasta with his 1958 Ford with a standard transmission and fitted with an axle hitch. I scoured the internet hoping I might find a picture of an antique axle hitch but had no luck. You would have loved it. This thing bolted to the rear axle of the Ford with hung U bolts and hung from the back bumper by chains. Go over a bump in the road and it would hit bottom. We went all over the United States with that rig.

After seven years dad was ready for something bigger. He had upgraded the Ford for a 1961 Dodge station wagon with an automatic push button transmission and of course BIG tail fins. The axle hitch was gone, scrapped and replaced with a hitch that was welded to the car. Just a note, welded hitches were the thing throughout the 1970s. Back to the trailer, dad set his sights on a 1966 Frolic. Among the upgrades in this travel trailer was a pressurized water system. Unlike today's systems the tank and lines were pressurized but there was no pump. The pressure came from my brother and I using a bicycle pump attached to a port on the tank. We would work for hours just to get enough water for mom to cook dinner and for us to wash up.

The Frolic only lasted two years and in 1968 dad bought his first Airstream. Finally we had a travel trailer with the amenities comparable to today's rigs; electric / battery lights, good size refrigerator, water pump (thank goodness), furnace and most important comfortable beds. Dad stayed with Airstreams for the rest of his traveling years progressing up to a 31 foot Airstream Excella before he quit traveling.

This brings us to when my adventures begin. In 1974 my wife and I made our first camping trip in a big 20 year old tent. When it was over I said never again and went out and purchased my first previously enjoyed trailer, a 1961 Reliart Popup which I paid $200 for. This was nothing more than beds on wheels with a free standing table. The box was 8'x8' and when opened was sixteen feet long. I pulled this gem with my 1974 Mustang. Was I a sight, but we were off the ground at night and could set it up in under five minutes. We kept that pop up until 1979 when I purchased a fifteen foot Scotty. My

Scotty had all the amenities of my father's first Shasta with the addition of a furnace and closet where I mounted a port-a-potty (my first modification). By now we had a second car, a 1977 Volare station wagon, which became my tow vehicle. The Scotty was twice the weight than I should have been pulling with the Volare but we never had problems. We didn't get anywhere fast either. My wife's grandfather would travel with us and when I came to a hill he would sit in the back seat saying "You can do it. Do you want me to put my foot out the door and kick?". Despite that we went up and down the east coast of the United States multiple times and made great memories.

This brings me to 1986. The family had grown to four and the Scotty was just too small so the wife and I purchased a 22 ½ foot Fleetwood Resort bunkhouse model. We kept that trailer for 20 years and it looked like new when I traded it in. My one big modification in the Resort was the addition of a cabinet over the second table and a microwave oven. In those days no-one had a microwave in their trailer and was I the talk of the town.

In 2007 my lifelong dream of owning a motorhome came true and we got a brand new Forest River Georgetown. I loved that coach and planned to have it well into retirement but, there is always a but. In 2008 Forest River came out with the

Berkshire product. It was a big shinny diesel pusher with four slides that I just had to have. If you remember, 2008 was a bad year for the RV industry. I got my Berkshire for half price as well as getting exactly what I paid for the Georgetown in trade. I bought the Berkshire 600 miles away from home and closed on it Christmas eve. That story is a book in itself as my wife and son will tell you. As of the writing of this book I still have the Berkshire, looks as new as the day it came off the production line and is now loaded with extras that I installed. So let's stop reminiscing and get on with the tweaks, modifications, and updates.

I almost forgot. If you would like to see pictures of the RVs my dad and I have owned, just look at the collage on the front cover. Not one of these rigs was maintained by anyone other than my father or me. As each was like new when we traded them in is a testament to our knowledge and expertise.

I talk about many products in this book. These discussions should not be considered endorsements of any kind. They are just products I have chosen to use. There may be other products that can do the same job. I just like the ones I have chosen. Now on with the tweaks, modifications, and updates.

SECTION 1: LIGHTING

LEDs

One of the easiest and most cost effective modifications you can do to your RV is to replace all the incandescent interior lights with LEDs. The advantage of LEDs is that they use much less power thus extending your battery life when boon docking. They will last tens of thousands of hours longer than incandescent. An LED bulb will probably never need to be replaced. They run cool so you will not get the heat buildup that incandescent lights cause making them safer. I have seen several melted incandescent light fixtures in my day. These could have caused a fire if not tended to. When changing out incandescent light fixtures, I have seen ever so many discolored ceilings caused by heat buildup. A very sobering sight.

In this topic I plan to discuss six bulb types. Those with a 921 base, those with an 1141 base, those that look like fuses, bulbs for the vanity and replacements for fluorescent bulbs. If you go to an RV show you can find any of these types of bulbs and will probably spend $15.00 or more for just one. You will be told how superior the bulb is and that it is specially designed to not cause TV interference. If you ask me they are the same bulbs I get from China and the only thing special about them is the markup the seller is asking you to pay. My rule of thumb is to spend less than $1.00 per bulb, unless it is a special configuration. I have never had problems with longevity or TV interference with the bulbs I have purchased.

These are your 921 type bulbs. There are several LED replacements but I like this type. If you were to search eBay or Amazon you would be looking for "LED Bulbs 6000k Super White / 3500K Warm white 3020". You can easily find 20 of these for $15.00.

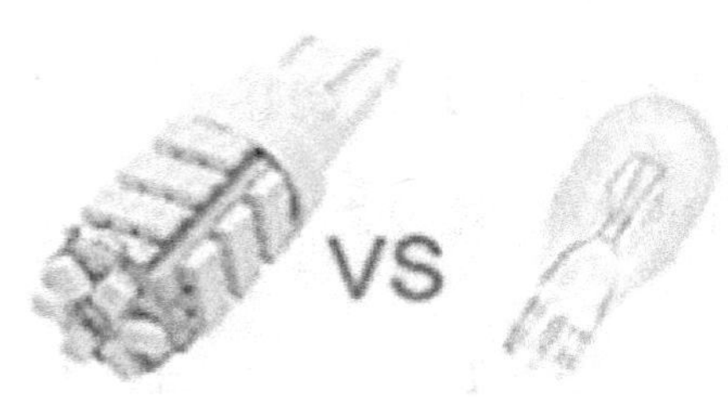

These are your 1141 type bulbs. I like the one depicted to the right. I have found these for as little as $13.00 for ten bubs and would search eBay or Amazon for "Warm White 1156 BA15S / 1141 / 1073 / 1095 Base 18 SMD 5050 LED Replacement Bulb For RV Camper SUV MPV Car Turn Tail Signal Brake Backup Light MA241"

This is a specialty type bulb used in the reading light shown. I had a devil of a time finding them but finally came upon one on eBay. Search for "Indoor Vehicles 1156 Ba15s SMD LED Bulbs Lighting SUNSET WHITE in 280 LUMEN" I have found these for as little as $45.00 for ten and as much as $15.00 each.

This fuse type bulb is used in my step well lights and isle lighting. I found these on eBay by searching for "Dome License Plate Light Bulbs". Two bulbs set me back $3.00.

This is a vanity light replacement found at Camping World for $13.00. A little pricy but it is the cheapest I have found. We do not use the vanity much so I am waiting for this price to come down before I replace them.

The "600 Lumen White LED Replacement Panels for Fluorescent Lights, 2-Pack". Another Camping World find for $35.00. About the same price for two fluorescent bulbs but only change it once. This draws just 1 amp of current from your RV supply.

This was an idea I had to help conserve power when boon docking. A strip of LEs lights along the top of our kitchen slide. Easily accomplished with a five meter roll of white LEDs, a dimmer on off switch, and 12 volt plug. The install makes them appear like indirect lighting when on and when off they cannot be seen.

The LEDs I used were "Cool white 5M 5050 300 LD ip65 waterproof Strip lights 60 LEDs / Meter Flexible". I like the 5050 style LEDs as they are brighter than others.

I always purchase the waterproof type so that I can dust the top of the slide with a damp cloth and not have to worry about shorting out or damage to the LEDs. The roll of LEDs is self adhering and can be cut every three inches making it easy to customize.

I used 16 gauge speaker wire to run the power line down the side of the slide then in under the kitchen counter. Once under the counter I found plenty of power as all the slide wiring comes to one point at the back corner prior to routing into the main RV. Most slides are designed in this manner.

The switch can be affixed in any convenient spot and is a "LED Dimmer Controller Single Color Bright Adjustable 12-24V For LED Light Strip".

The 12 volt connector is simply a "12 Volt Connector".   I got all the parts on eBay. Just search for the quoted names I have provided.

To ensure everything stays in place I put a dab of clear GE silicon every six inches along the LED strip and the wire that was run down the back side of the slide trim. This whole modification cost me $20.00 as I had the speaker wire and silicone.

If you need to purchase wire it can be found at any box store for $15.00 and the silicone for about $5.00.

UNDER CUPBOARD COLOR CHANGING ACCENT LIGHTS

Add Stunning accent lighting anywhere in your RV.

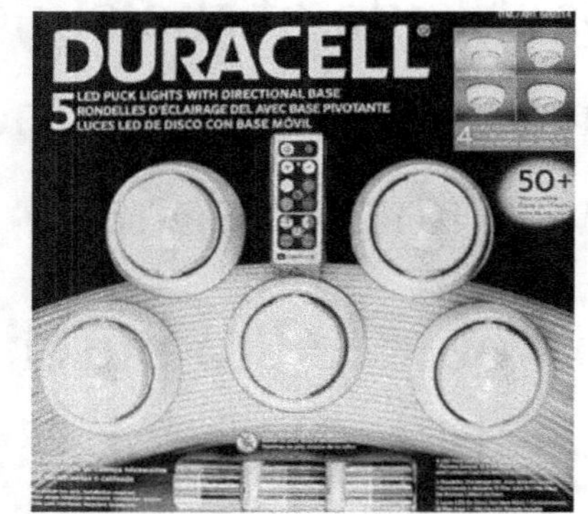

These lights give you the power to change colors (up to 12) and more.

Each light is wireless and can be controlled with the included remote so you can place them anywhere just peal and stick.

The lights are battery operated (15 batteries included) so there is no wiring required.

Lights may be found at
http://www.pulsetv.com/prodinfo.asp?number=7808

Or

https://www.amazon.com/Capstone-Puck-Lights-Directional-Count/dp/B071GGKVQC/ref=pd_sbs_60_3?_encoding=UTF8&psc=1&refRID=9JTFYYJ4W6B7PKJ3Y74W

PORCH LIGHT or SCARE LIGHT

I have had one of these installed on my coach (see picture to right) since the summer of 2012 and I think they are great. If you walk by my coach after dark you would noticed the porch light come even if no one is in the coach. I feel this is a great security product for a low cost. No matter where you are parked the last thing a thief or someone out for mischief wants is a spot light to come on highlighting what they are up to. Designed to install in the same holes your current porch light is mounted in and use the same wiring this is an easy upgrade. The product name is **<u>STARLIGHT</u>** and depending on the type, color, and LED or incandescent bulb type can be had for anywhere from $35 to $65.

Additional capabilities are

Can function as a regular porch light

Motion Detection Function- and equipped with microchip that distinguishes between people and small animals or blowing debris

Daylight Sensor- turns light off during daylight hours

Monitor alerts you when your battery is low

Has capability to control additional lighting

Can replace OEM round or rectangular porch lights.

Other styles of STARLIGHTS available are in either black or white.. To find them search for Starlight.

LED PATIO LIGHTING

This was one of the first modifications I performed on my Berkshire motorhome. It was born out of the need to have better patio lighting and add some glitz to the coach. This was accomplished with a roll of RGB LEDs, a remote control unit, and 12 volt power brick. All three items

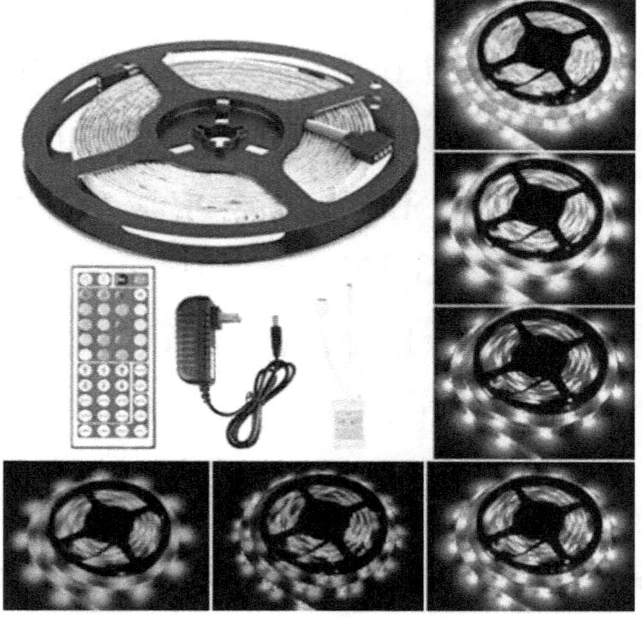

can be found in one kit by searching Amazon. When selecting the kit I looked specifically for 5050 style LEDs in rolls of 60 LEDs per meter and made sure they are the water proof type. For installation the roll of LEDs is self adhering and can be cut every three inches making it easy to fit. Note: be sure to save the leftover strip of LEDs as I have a use for it later in this book.

I mounted the LEDs under my slide rather than under the coach. My thought process is they will be protected from road debris while traveling. Many people have asked me how I could mount the LEDs under the slide and not have them crushed when the slid is retracted. Every slide has about a three inch zone at the very edge that is free of slide hardware and so the LEDs come in contact with nothing. I placed the LEDs under both the kitchen and wardrobe slides on the passenger side of the coach. This gave me light the total length of the coach.

I simply drilled a ½ inch hole and routed the end of the LED strip through the hole into the coach. In the picture I use duct tape to cover the hole. I found that this dried out however and need to be replaced every year. I have since replaced the tape with a piece of plastic cut from a coffee can lid and screwed to the bottom of the slide to cover the hole. The IR senior is positioned at the edge of the plastic cover.

Once inside under the kitchen counter and wardrobe slide I found plenty of power as all the slide wiring comes to one point at the back corner of the slide prior to routing into the main RV. Most slides are designed in this manner. I installed an outlet box and AC outlet in each slide. Then plugged in the power and the IR receiver into the power brick and RGB LED slide strip.

On newer installs I have omitted the power brick and tied directly into the RVs 12 volt system. This lets LEDs be used whether plugged into AC or not. With the remote control I can program the LEDs to any color in the rainbow or make them display in different patterns. They give the coach a great look and I get a lot of compliments.

To ensure everything stays in place I put a dab of clear GE silicon every six inches along the LED strip. This whole modification cost me $20.00 for each set of LEDs, remote, and power brick. I used two sets.

LED LIGHTING UPGRADE

Since installing my LED Lighting an RF remote controller has become available. The IR is still more common when purchasing bundles but if you look you can find the RF type. I changed mine so I could turn the LEDs on and not have to be in direct line of sight of the IR sensor. Below I have listed several RF controllers I have found that work well. Search the internet for the name and you should be able to fine them.

"FAVOLCANO ini LED Controller Dimmer with 11 Key RF Wireless Remote Control DC 5~24V 12A for Single Color 3528 5050 LED Strip Lights" This two wire device would be used to run the inside accent LEDS.

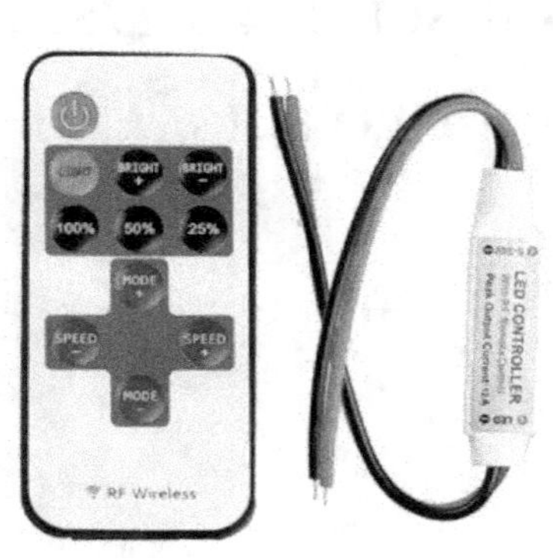

"RGBZONE DC 5V-24V 12A RGB LED Controller with 17-key RF Wireless Remote Control Dimmer for 5050 3528 5630 LED Strip Lights" This is what I am now running my under slide LED with.

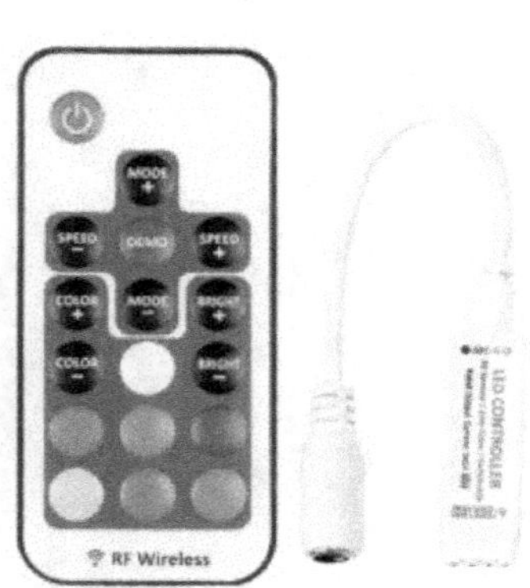

Here we have a manual RGV compact controller. "RGBZONE DC 12V Mini 3 Key LED Controller 12V Switch ON/OFF Dimmer for 5050 3528 5630 RGB LED Strip Light". No remote but a manual controller.

LED ISLE LIGHTING

We often take the grandchildren camping with us and one thing that is missing in the front sleeping area of the coach is a night light. From that  came the idea for LED isle lighting. The kids love them and always ask grandpa to turn on the circus lights. They also love to play with them changing the colors and making them go through patterns. I like them as isle/night lighting, the original purpose. At bedtime I program them to a soft blue and turn down the brightness.

This modification was accomplished using the left over LED string I cut off from the patio light installation. I then purchased an RF remote as I discussed in the LED LIGHTING UPGRADE Chapter. I tied these into a 12 volt DC power line I found under the kitchen cabinets. Remember as I have stated before the manufacturer ran all the electrical to the back corner of the slide prior to routing into the coach. Just explore and you can find the wires then identify the 12 volt and ground wires.

As I have done before, to ensure everything stays in place I put a dab of clear GE silicon every six inches along the LED strip. This whole modification cost me $6.00, the cost of the LED controller.

The material I used is pictured below. Please see LED PATTIO LIGHTING, ACCIENT LIGHTING INSIDE THE RV, and LED UPGRADE chapters to learn where to purchase each item.

A new RGB kit or scrap from Patio lighting install

RF LED controller is using left over LEDs

12 Volt power connectors and 16 gauge speaker wire.

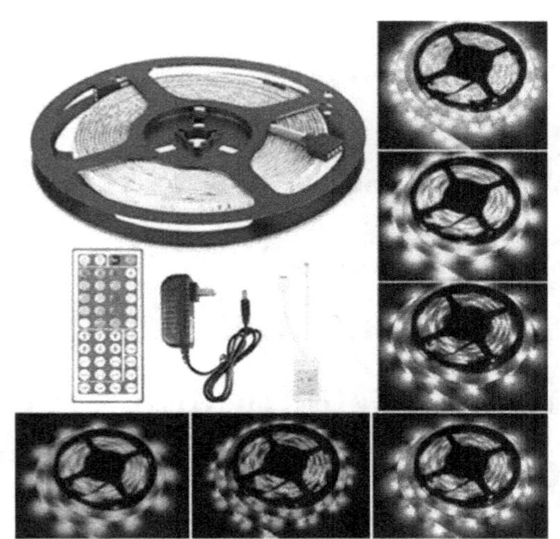

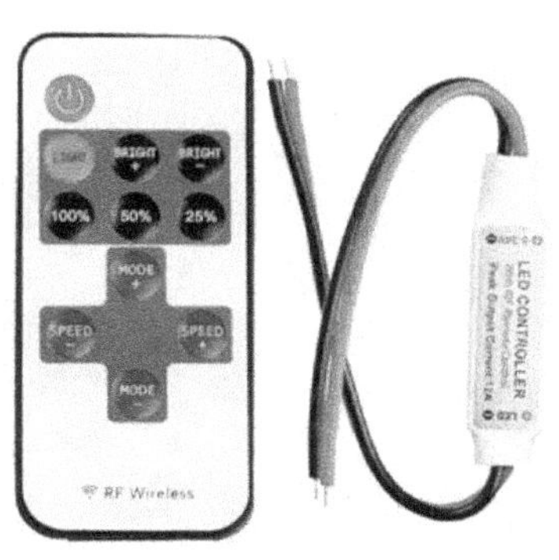

LED CLOSET LIGHT

Do you have a dark closet? What about one of these? I found this on the Camping World site for $15.00 Light activates when the door is open and turns off when the door is closed. Led runs cool to reduce the chance of a fire.

Another solution is this found at Job Lot stores. It is called the "Great RV Closet Light" This runs on batteries and sticks to the wall with double sided tape. This little gem throws a lot of light. Information can be found here

http://roselawnlutheran.org/decor/great-rv-led-closet-light/

If you performed the upgrade described in the ACCENT LIGHTING, INSIDE THE RV chapter then this upgrade could be free. It was for me.

If you look in the basement of my coach you will see one light at the top of the cabinet then two shelves. We use this cabinet as our pantry and after dark the one top light does not illulinate the entire area. The solution was to use two sections of the left over white LED strip lights from the ACCENT LIGHTING upgrade and connect them to the light the manufacture provided. When that light is turned on the LEDs also turn on. Simple and cheep.

As I have done before, to ensure everything stays in place I put a dab of clear GE silicon every six inches along the LED strip.

RV CHANDELIER

How about an LED Chandelier? This cute idea can be mounted on any roof vent? Another Camping world find for only $15.00. Remove the original vent surround and install this one. Tie it into 12 Volt line found in most RV vent openings and you have an instant chandelier. I did this with a friends RV. The only thing you need to add is the on /off switch.

If you have ever arrived at your destination after dark you know that backing into a site can be difficult if there is poor lighting. I got tired of this and finally installed LED Driving Lights at the back of my coach. They are  controlled by a toggle switch with a lighted handle. The handle light is so I will not leave the lights on. A sort of reminder for an old man.

The main question I get regarding this upgrade is where did I run the wiring? I have a diesel pusher motorhome built on a Freightliner XC chassis.

Down the side of each rail on this chassis are routing conduits that Freightliner uses to route wires and hoses from the front to back of the coach.

Using an electrical snake I routed a length of 16 gauge speaker wire the length of the coach.

I would like to note that anytime I route wires through the coach I also parallel a run of mason twine. This is a very strong string. I do this so in the future if I need another wire run in the same place I do not have to re-snake the path.

After routing through the conduit I took the speaker wire and wove it along the hinge on the

back engine hatch so that I could open it with the lights in place.

 At the front of the coach I routed the wire into the power compartment on the driver's side of the coach. From there I connected to a

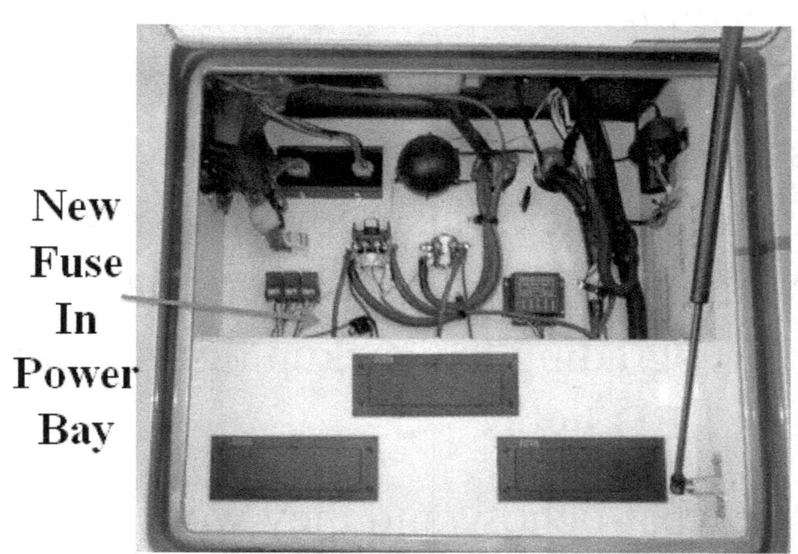

fuse then found power.   I then routed the hot wire into the coach following the path the manufacture used for his wires and up to the switch which I mounted in the dash.

Cost of this upgrade was about $50. Materials were the running lights, user preference. A lighted switch found on eBay, 16 gauge speaker wire found at one of the big box stores, and a fuse holder found on eBay.

BACKUP LIGHTS REV TWO

After having my rear driving lights installed for several years I found the need for an additional set of lights under the coach chassis. Not wanting to run another wire from the front of the coach to the back I just moved my rear driving lights down. This left me without light when backing in after dark. I solved this by upgrading the backup lights on my coach to 1200 lumens LED lights.

This is what I chose and they work great. Cost was $17.00.

AUXITO

AUXITO 1200 Lumens 3157 LED Bulbs Extremely Bright 48-SMD 4014 LED Chipsets 3156 3057 4057 4157 LED Bulbs with Projector for Backup Reverse Lights, 6000K Xenon White (Pack of 2)

LIGHT FOR DOOR HANDLE

Do you have this type of door handle on your RV? It was designed to be lit yet some manufactures choose not to install the bulb. If yours is one you can do the install yourself.

Search for "ITC (86430-LED ASSEM-DB) Cool White Replacement LED Light Assembly for IllumaGrip Handles" on Amazon or go to web address

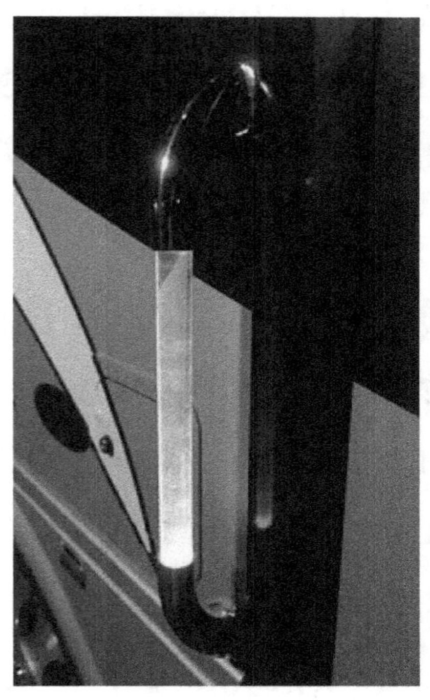

https://www.amazon.com/gp/product/B00K779EH6/ref=oh_aui_detailpage_o00_s01?ie=UTF8&psc=1

If you are lucky the manufacture may have wired the power to the handle just not installed the light.

LIGHTED DOOR HANDLE REV II

What if you want a lighted door handle but do not have a power source by the door or do not have one of those fancy glass handles? Look to the right.

"20.75" IllumaGrip Battery Operated Safety Handle operates on 4 AA rechargeable batteries (included) with an estimated life of 1-month at 24/7 operation" for $56.00. Simple to install.

This is the perfect solution. Runs on four AA batteries and can be mounted anywhere. Has a day / night sensor so install it and forget it.

PANTRY LIGHTING

Once I built our kitchen pantry we found it difficult to see things in it due to the dark narrow deep nature of the cupboard. The solution I thought of was to line the cupboard with the same type of LED lights I used to install along the inside of the kitchen slide (the accent lights). "Cool White 5M 5050 300 LED ip65 waterproof Strip Lights 60 LEDs/Meter". Rather than having to flip a switch to turn the lights on and off I installed a pin switch on the door. This turns the lights on automatically any time the door is opened and off when closed. I found power in the basement of the coach and ran a length of 16 gauge speaker wire to connect to them.

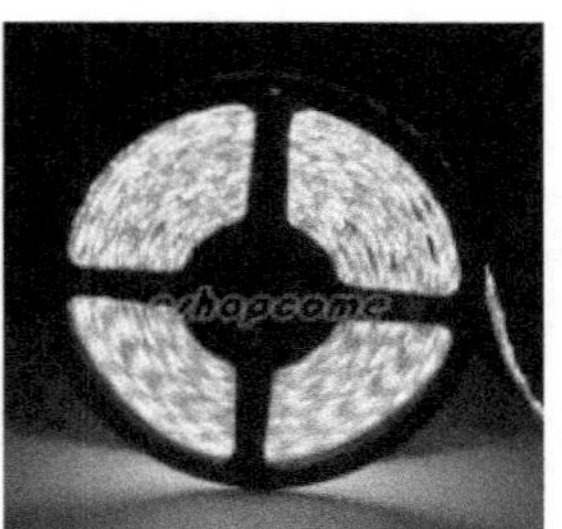

This whole modification cost about $15.00

SECTION 2: SAFETY and SECURITY

THIRD TAIL LIGHT

A few years ago on my way home from an international RV rally I had an opportunity to follow several different motorhomes. One thing that stood out on these coaches was how noticeable the third tail light on the back was. I began to think that this was a real safety feature and I should have one. On my return home I went on Amazon and found this for $23.00 CCIYU 15 Waterproof Red Sealed 11 LED Light Bar Truck Trailer RV Stop Turn Tail 3rd Brake Light (Pack of 2 pcs).

The back cap of my motorhome is hollow which made them easy to install. I drilled one ½ inch hole for each light to route the wires then just screwed the 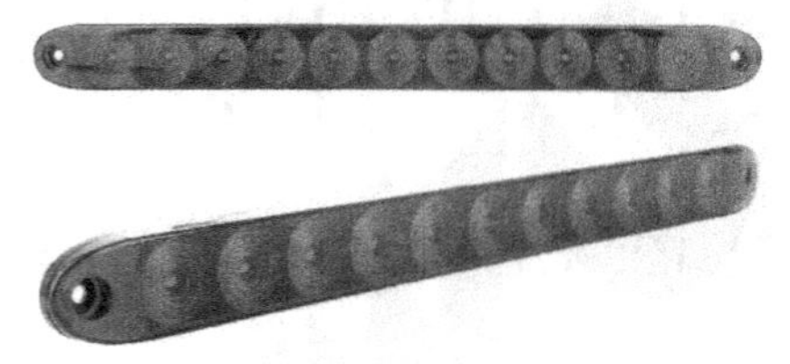 lights on. Once mounted I simply removed the tail light on each side of the coach, reached in and connected the third tail light to the coach lights.

SOLUTIONS FOR LOST KEYS

Are you ever worried about losing your keys, walking out of the RV and inadvertently locking the door with your keys inside, or just do not want to carry your keys around at the campground? I saw this idea, loved it, and installed it in my coach and several others coaches of friends.

A key lock box as is used in the real-estate industry. They can be had for as little as $15 and come in many different styles. You can purchase a box that can be permanently installed to a frame member or a box that mimics a padlock and can be installed around a pipe or some other object. Hiding places for these boxes could be your propane storage, under the RV frame, or in a cabinet you do not lock. Get a combination box and use your phone number, last four digits of your Social Security number or any other number that is easy to remember as the combination. This provides a secure way to have access to spare keys. Lock boxes can be purchased on Amazon or any of the big box stores.

I have the one displayed at the left. The pictures to the right shows a padlock style box.

Additional features for these lock boxes are

Lockbox provides sturdy and secure keyless access.

Choose your own code that you will remember.

Has enough storage for an entire ring of keys.

Tough and strong.

Below is a picture on one installed in a propane cupboard on a motorhome.

KEYLESS DOOR LOCK

When I get to the campground I hate carrying my keys around. On top of this, shortly after purchasing my Berkshire I heard that the company uses only five different door keys for the entire fleet. Not believing this I went up to a buddy's Berkshire and for a lark tried my key. IT WORKED! Another upgrade/modification had just been born.

There are several excellent keyless entry systems available on the market that swap out for the original RV door lock. Their price normally begin at $300 and goes up after that. I looked into these products but not only was the price a discouragement none were made to replace my style lock. Another solution was needed. I turned to the home market and found a keyless entry door lock for just under $100.00. It had the two options I felt I must have. The first was a remote and second a key backup in the event the lock malfunctions or the batteries fail.

As my RV door is 2 inches thick a conventional lock would not work. They are designed for 1 ½ inch doors. An insert plate that I had a buddy fabricate reduced the lock area to 1 ½ inches.

Next I set to cutting a hole in the door and mounting the lock. I used a 2 inch hole saw for the outside hole and a vibrating multi tool for the inside hole.

I mounted the lock upside down which allows me to access the dead bolt on the inside through the sliding door/window in the screen door.

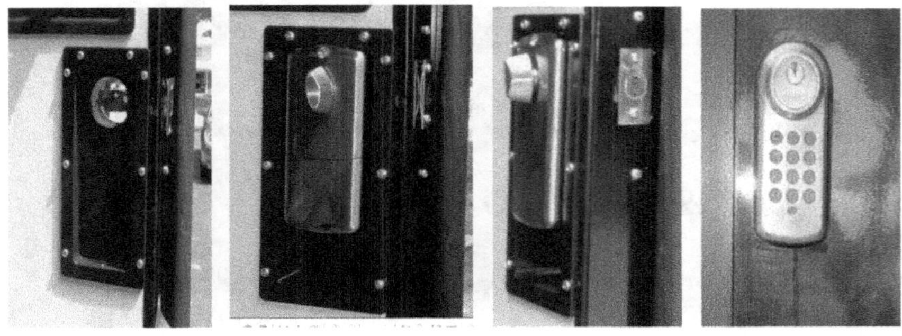

I have had this lock installed since 2102 and it has worked perfectly. The only maintenance I perform is to change the batteries every spring.

When I purchassed my lock back in 2102 I got it from one of the big box stores. They carry locks for standard size doors only. Through doing this modificstion for friends I have learned that they make locks that can be used on thick doors. These eliminate the need for the insert plate and only require a hole saw and drill to install. Much easier.

NEW KEY CORES

Back in 2012 while attending the FMCA international show in Indanapolis I came across the TriMark booth. They were offering to recore RV locks so that you would have a unique key for both the basement locks and the entry door. The cost for this service was $75.00 and included 12 new cores and two keys.

>> TriMark Europe is planning to show its KeyOnePlus system, a mechanical lock and key combination that enables users to choose keys from a range more than 1,000 key codes, designed to eliminate the security problems caused by the traditional "one key fits all" issue with construction equipment that makes it easy to steal.

TriMark called this their "key one plus" system. I have never seen it since so am glad I got it when I did.

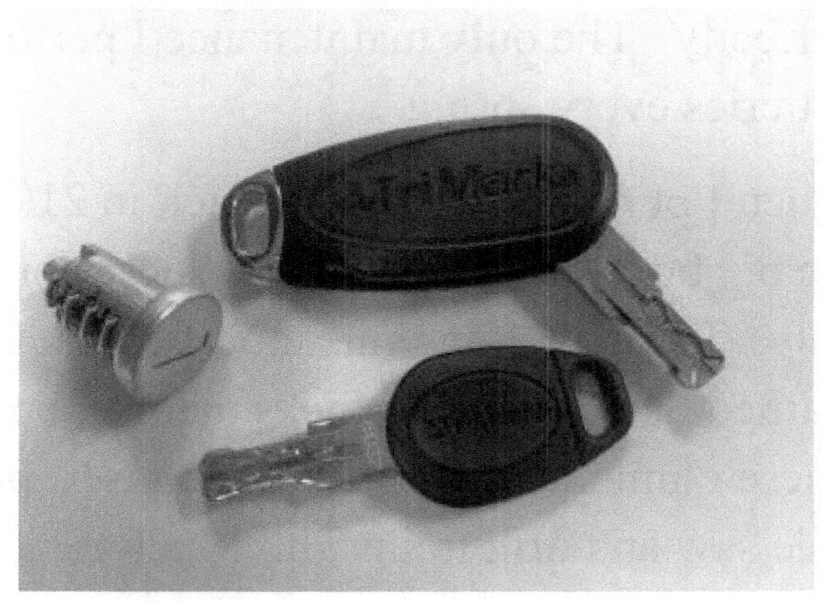

Chassis Camera, what is it, why do I need one, and why have I included it under safety?

A chassis camera is just what the name implies. It is a camera mounted under the coach that lets me watch the rear chassis of the motorhome.

Why is this important? My diesel pusher and many others are very low to the ground. This results in the back of the motorhome dragging on hills or when entering roads that are separated by culverts. The camera allows me to see when this is going to happen and adjust the coach speed the path to prevent it.

My first evolution of this was a Peak wireless backup camera. The monitor was mounted on the dash and the camera mounted on my mud flap frame. The instructions for these types of cameras say tap power off the reverse lights but I wanted to use the camera while driving forward and in reverse. To solve this

I tapped power from the hot line in the trailer tow plug on the back of the motorhome.

In my case this line is relay controlled and only hot when the key is on. Perfect, the camera will operate while the coach is in operation but be turned off when the coach is off. This way the battery will not draw down when the coach is sitting.

My motorhome is forty feet long and when I mounted the camera transmitter under the back of the coach the monitor showed a lot of snow. The signal could not penetrate the coach and reach the monitor. This was solved by bring the transmitter into the rear closet at the back inside. I did this by drilling a ½ inch hole in the floor of the closet that allowed me to rout the transmitter wiring down to the camera. This worked prefect, clear sharp picture.

An added benefit of this system is when I have the toad attached I can see the connections and wire harness which provides a little more piece of mind when towing.

The Peak system I had is no longer available but a comparable system can be found here. Cost will vary from $100.00 to $150.00

https://www.amazon.com/Peak-PKC0BU7-Wireless-7-Inch-Back-up/dp/B009VYWJ0A/ref=sr_1_2?ie=UTF8&qid=1510347270&sr=8-2&keywords=peak+backup+camera&dpID=51icETNLbBL&preST=_SX300_QL70_&dpSrc=srch

CHASSIS CAMERA REV TWO

As time passed and I purchased more toys and the dash of the coach began to get crowded. A solution was needed. One of the items I had on the dash was my RandMcnally 7730 GPS. This GPS has provisions for a camera input. I removed the Peak system and purchased the necessary hardware to impliment my chassis camera using the 7730.

Parts needed were a camera and a means to get the camers signal up to the 7730.   I purchased a "170°Anti Fog Glass Car Auto Rear View Reverse Backup Waterproof CMOS Camera" for $12.99 and a "2.4GHZ RCA Wireless Transmitter Receiver Kit Set for Car Rearview Camera" for $12.92. I found both of these on eBay.

Having had to be towed due to a breakdown I learned mounting the camera to the coach mud flap bracket was not   wise. A good tow operator will remove the mud flap to prevent damage during the tow so the camera would have to be disconnected. I therefore fashioned a bracket on the back of the coach to which the camera is mounted. This can be seen below.

The picture on this system is nice and clear just like the Peak system. To make it work I just tap the camera icon on the GPS.

UPRGADE DASH CAMERA SYSTEM

My Berkshire is an early 2008 model. Back then the manufacture did not install side cameras and only used black and white rear camers. My dash entertainment system is a ASA VR187. On researching this system I learned it was capable of supporting color cameras as well as side cameras that would switch on automatically with the directional lights. The cameras used with the VR187 are Voyager cameras. If you are familare with these cameras they are very good but also very expensive. One camera costs $399,00 and the connection cables cost $75.00. To install two side cameras and upgrade the back camer to color would normally cost over $1300.00, WOW!

I learned that if you shop the internet late in the year and early spring you can find dealers unloading last year's voyager invetory for a fraction of new cost. I was able to perform my entire upgrade for only $262.00. Quite a cost difference from the $1300.00

 I have upgraded four coaches since for a simular cost.

The upgrade process:

First the back camera, The new color is plug and play compatable with the old black and white so the swap is easy. Remove the old black and white camera and install the color camera in the reverse order.

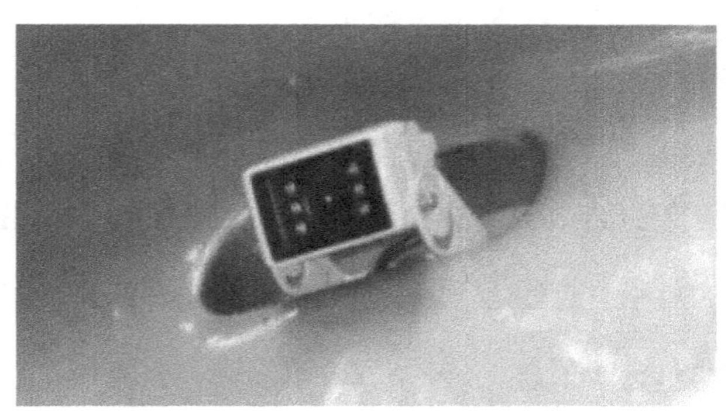

The side cameras were another matter. As I never had cameras to begin with new video cables had to be run and camera mounts made.

A ¾ inch hole was drilled into each side of the coach positioned so that they came out behind the front dash. The video wires were routed from the back of the VR187 to the holes, the camera mounts were screwed to the coach over the holes, cameras connect to the cables and installed. The connections on the back of the VR187 are well identified so it was very easy to see where to connect the cables. Below are the results.

CCTV SYSTEM WITH FOUR CHANNEL DVR

This was by far the most technical challenging and time consuming upgrade I have performed. It took two weeks to complete.

My trip to UTAH highlighted the need for some kind of camera system while driving. On the two lane highways out west there are so many drivers that will pull out to pass then wait for the last minute to get back to their lane. Additionally RVs are always being cut off. While a dash cam is one solution it will not capture activity behind you or on your side. I felt these views were equally as important as the front view. This is why I went with a CCTV system with the four channel DVR over a simple dash cam. While driving I can record everything, 360 degrees around me. As a bonus I can use the system while parked as a security system.

My system will record 62 hours of video and audio on one SIM card.

Back in 2014 when I installed this system there were not too many around, so I had to configure it myself. Today you can purchase complete packages for as little as $300.00 to $400.00. You will want to search the internet for Bus DVR systems. One I saw that looked interesting can be found here https://www.amazon.com/TrackSec-Channel-Mobile-Recorder-G-sensor/dp/B019AW88ZM/ref=sr_1_23?s=digital-text&ie=UTF8&qid=1511391019&sr=8-23&keywords=Bus+camera+system

The components I choose for my system were the DVR unit itself. "CCTV 4CH ReaMini ltime SD Card Mobile Bus Car Vehicle DVR Recorder System Audio".

Not only will this unit act as a recorder but if you wish you can set up triggers to your directional lights and backup light switch so the views on the monitor will change automatically.

I chose a system that used a SIM card to store the video rather than hard drive . I was concerned what road vibrations might do to the hard drive. If choosing today I would get one that did support a hard drive for storage and install an SSD drive. A configuration with an SSD drive could store months of video versis my 62 hours and no vibration issues.

I chose a 9 inch monitor that turns itself on when it senses power (key on). The big reason for the large

size is I keep all four cameras displaied while driving.

While I did not choose these cameras if specifing today I would. "CAIRUTE® Universal Mini CCD High Definition Night Vision 360 Degree Car Rear Front Side View Backup Camera With Mirror Image Conversion Lines"

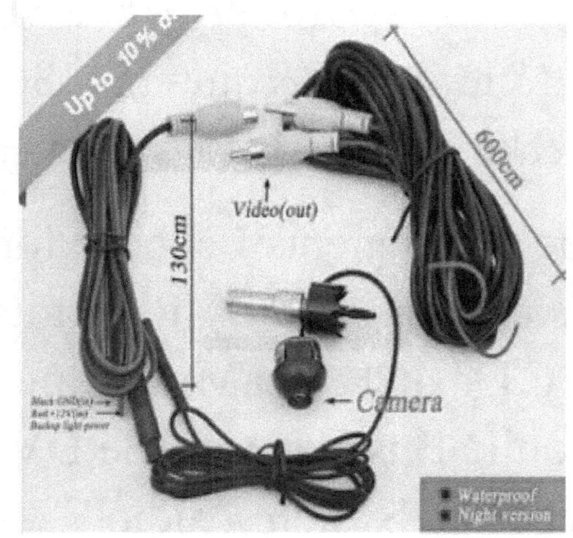

The cameras are the same form factor and specifications as I have but have the added ability to mirror the image. This is importanf as the two side cameras and back camera need to be on mirror mode. For that I needed different cameras. The cameras come with a hole saw so the mounting hole is perfict.

The microphone is "Outdoor Waterproof Adjustable Sensibility Audio Pickup Advanced Mic for DVR" This is mounted in at the front of the coach to catch any conversations.

"Car Boat SPST Blue LED Light 12V 20A Tip Toggle ON/OFF Switch" Lighted switch to turn the system on and off.

Mounting the hardware at the front of the coach was straight forward. Select a location for the cameras and microphone drill holes using the provided hole saw and mount the hardware. By opening the generator compartment I could easly route the wires and take them into the cab through a firewall plug.

The rear camera was a little more work. I have a diesel pusher motorhome built on a Freightliner XC chassis.

Down the side of each rail on this chassis are routing troths that Freightliner use to route wires and hoses from the front to back of the coach. Using an electrical snake I routed a length of 16 gauge speaker wire the length of the coach. I would like to note that anytime I route wires through the coach I also parallel a run of mason twine. This is a very strong string. I do this so if in the future I need another wire run the same place I do not have to re snake it. I took the speaker wire and wove it along the hinge on the back engine hatch so that I could open it with the camera in place. I then chose a location for the camera, drilled the hole, mounted and connected the wires.

Inside the coach I mounted the DVR under the dash. The instructions call for the DVR to be connected to a constant power line and the ignition. I connected the DVR through the optional switch to power and used my radio power switch to simulate the ignition. This allows me to run the system while parked as well as driving.

To follow are pictures of the installation.

First, the monitor showing the four views then the DVR and the camera mounts. Note: the side cameras are mounted to shoot under the slides when they are extended and the back camera will function with the engine hatch open or closed.

Next a view of the DEV installed and the lighted power switch.

The front camera is mounted in the nose of the coach, just
below the center of the windshield.

The side cameras are the small buttons below the side dash system cameras.

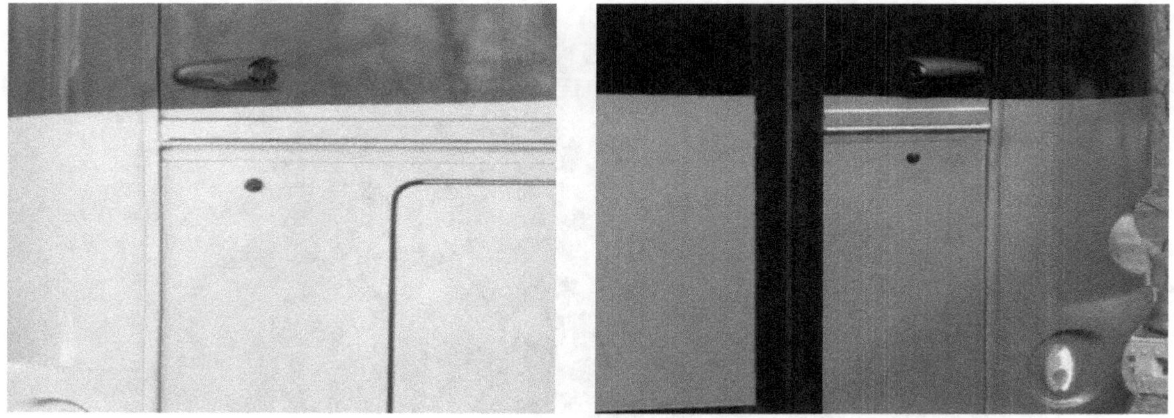

Last, the rear camera. I mounted it on the hatch so it will function with the hatch open or closed.

SECTION 3: RV INTERIOR

MEDICINE CABINET UPGRADE

I am constantly looking for a low cost solution to fix common RV problems. One that I have used often employs five gallon paint stir sticks. These are available at any of the large box stores for free. Just ask for them at the paint department. They are printed with the store name on one side but blank on the reverse side. I always keep a dozen on hand for quick fixes.

The first problem to be addressed is the RV medicine cabinet. We all have one and dutifully load it up with our tooth brush and tooth paste, aspirin, shampoo, and whatever. We drive to our campsite, have a great day, get ready for bed, open the medicine cabinet and out tumbles everything we have stored in there. Well a simple fix is to get a few Stir Sticks, Polly Stain to match the RV cabinet, some ½ inch number 6 screws, and a stubby screw driver. Stain the sticks to match the cabinet, cut to length, drill a hole in each end, and affix to the inside lip of the cabinet. They will act as a shelf guard. Problem solved. I have done this modification to many RVs and it works great.

What do you do when the medicine cabinet that came with the RV just is not large enough? How about turning the entire back of the bathroom door into a huge medicine cabinet?

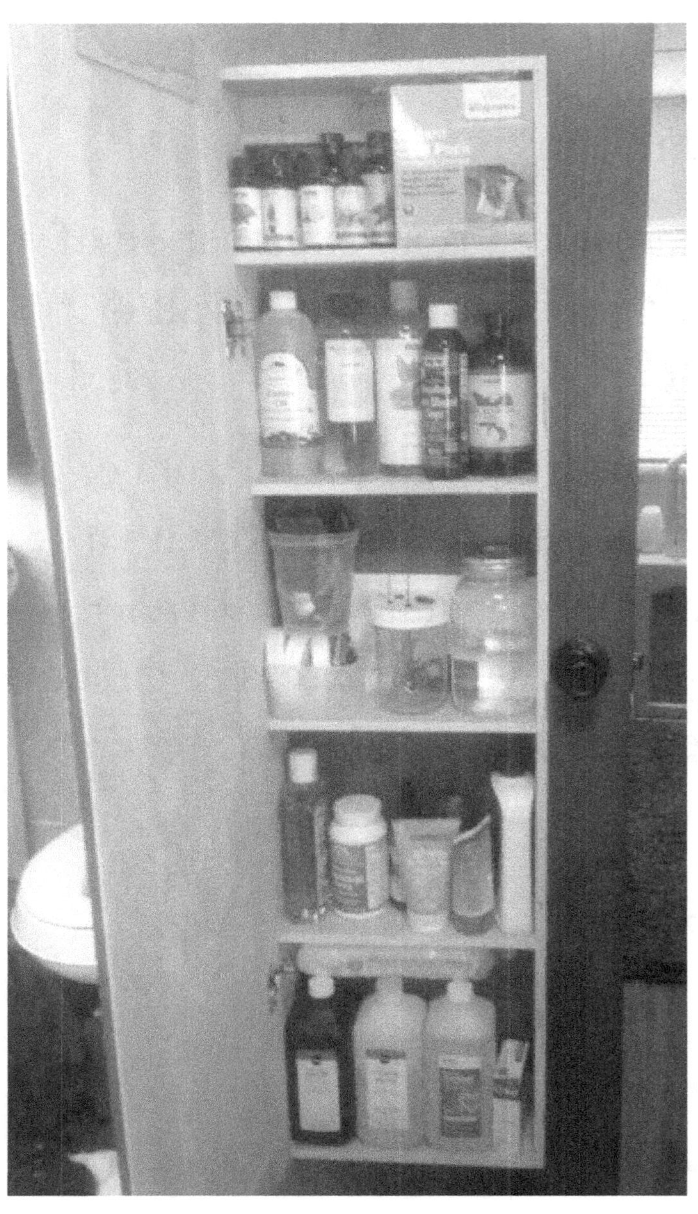

How is this accomplished?

You first go to a store such as WalMart and purchase a behind the door full length mirror for in the neighbor hood of $13.00. Then home to the wood working shop or to a handy friend who builds a cabinet around the mirror. Stain to match your RV interior and hang on the interior of the bathroom door with L brackets and well nuts.

This whole modification should not cost over $50.00.

At the risk of being redundant here again is an explanation of well nuts. They are great for holding items to s thin wall or roof and I use them a lot in the RV.

To use well nuts you drill a hole large enough for the rubber of the nut to fit through. Insert the nut into the hole and with a bolt about ¼ inch longer than the rubber t attach the towel bracket to the door face. The well nut will compress in the hole holding the bracket secure. Then attach the rod to the bracket.

Below is a nice graphic of how well nuts work. You will see this described over and over in the book as I am trying to have each section be stand alone. Sorry for the person reading the entire book.

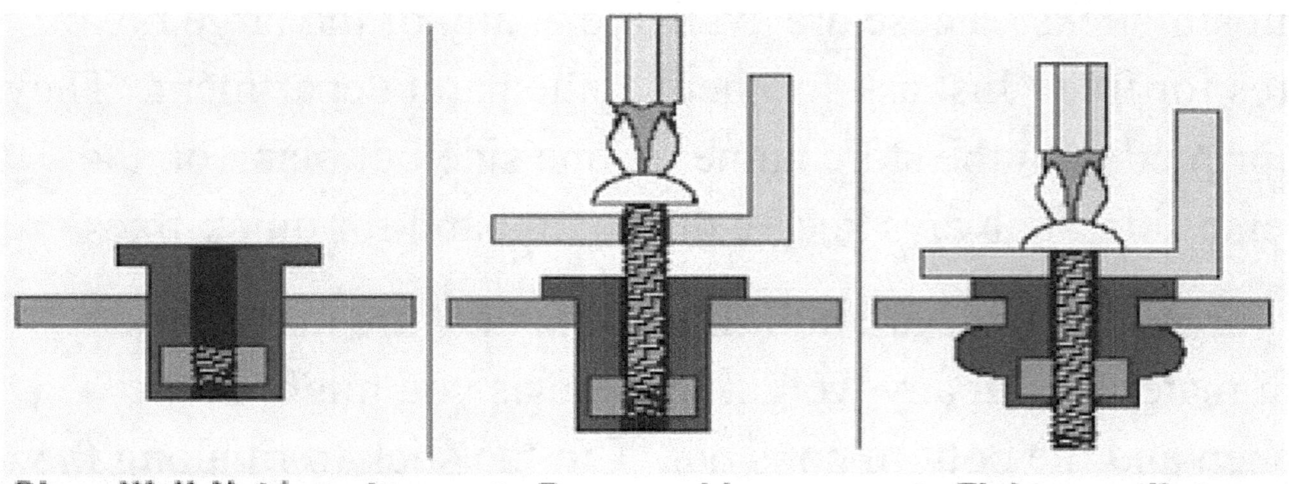

LOW COST DRAWER FIX

I am constantly looking for a low cost solution to fix common RV problems. One that I have used often employs five gallon paint stir sticks. These are available at any of the large box stores for free. Just ask for them at the paint department. They are printed with the store name on one side but blank on the reverse side. I always keep a dozen on hand for quick fixes.

If your RV drawers are built like mine they are made of very light material. Put any weight in them as you might in the kitchen and the bottom pops out. Cut the stick to fit along the bottom back of the drawer. Glue in place and hold with a couple of 1/2 inch number 6 screws shot through from the inside. Then make a bracket from any type of metal, even an old soda can and screw in place to prevent the back of the draw from bowing out. Again hold in place with flat head number 6 screws. Load the draw up as desired.

DRAWER WITHIN a DRAWER

This modification was done by a buddy and I thought it was neat.

Many RVs have one deep dray under the stove rather than two small drawers. Where does one keep the silverware in this situation? Install the drawer within a drawer modification.

The modification is accomplished by taking out the large drawer, take the front and rollers off, then carefully cut the existing box down the height which you want for the silverware tray. Put a bottom on the portion cut off and you have the basis for a new drawer. Now add dividers or purchase a silverware organizer and place in the new drawer. Add new roller slides on the new drawer and put it all together.

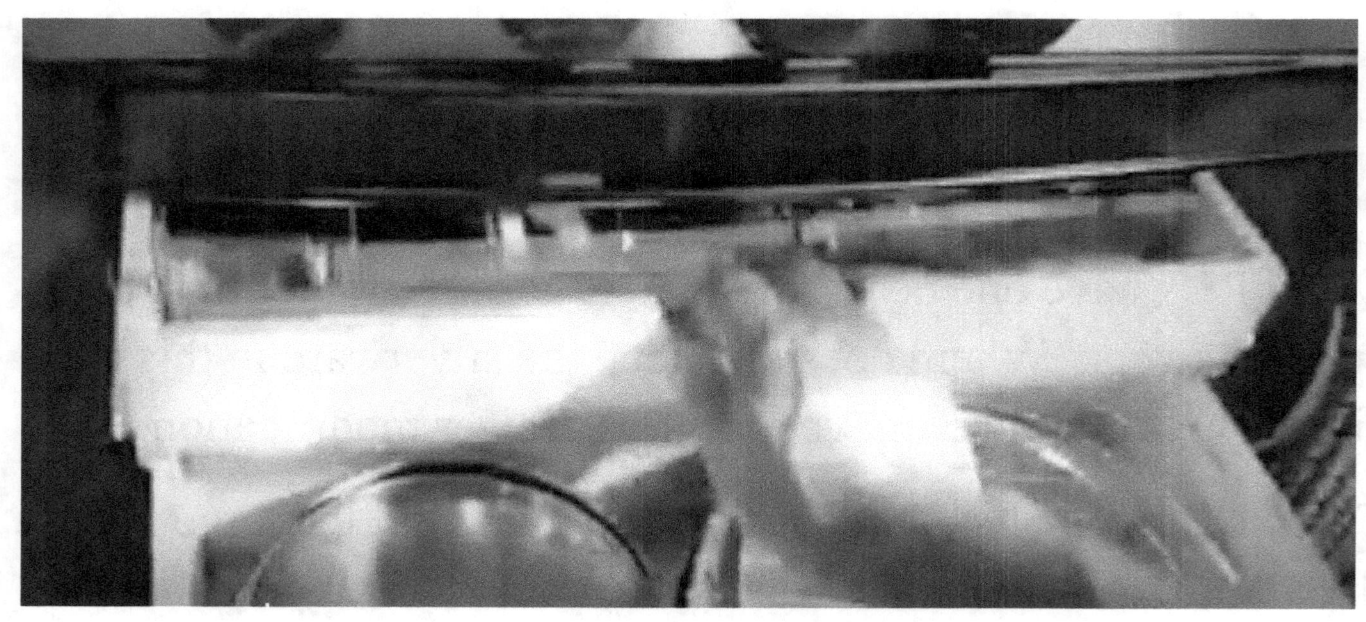

Next to our refrigerator we have this narrow tall cupboard that was just screaming for an upgrade. I thought it would make the perfect rifle cupboard but the wife had a different idea, thus our kitchen pantry was born.

Now this space is eight inches wide by three feet deep. Trying to install draw slides was next to impossible due to access to the back area. The solution was to make what I refer to as ladders. These ladders would frame out the cupboard, allow attachment of the draw slides outside the cupboard and then slide into the cupboard and are attached to the floor and ceiling with L brackets.

Next the drawers, I built these out of ¼ inch plywood and glued and tacked them together. In the front of each drawer I affixed a lock that not only would hold the drawer in but could be used as a pull. This whole project cost about $100.00 with all material available at the big box stores. The main cost was the drawer slides

To follow is a view of the completed project and a view of the combination drawer locks and pulls.

Back in 2008 as well as the country having a recession and all the bank failures that happened there must have been a wood shortage. I say this because my coach has all these wonderful big and deep cupboards with no shelves. Trying to organize them is next to impossible. To solve this I made draws and purchased a trash can organizer. The total cost of this modification was $200.00. This seems high but the trash can organizer alone was $160.00. This particular one was more than others but it fit my cabinet, came with the cans, and provided two bins so we can have garbage and recyclables.

All the materials were readily available at the big box store.

The boxes were simple to make. The sides are 3/4 inch birch with rabbits on the edges and a dado on the bottom for the floating floor. They are held together with wood glue and dry wall screws. When making the boxes be sure to subtract the width measurement of the chosen slides or the finished product will not fit.

Normally the slides will attach to the side of the cabinet but one of my cabinets has a floating floor. Under this floor is all the electric for the kitchen slide. Here I attached the slides to the floor of the cabinet using a piece of scrap wood. This allows the floor to continue to be removed for access to the wiring.

I normally use this type of slide as they are easy to install and low in price.

Below another view of the finished product stuffed with dog toys feeding bowls.

I should add that if you are not handy at wood working there are several people on eBay that will build custom drawers for a fair price. You need only provide the measurements.

ORGANIZE THE ENTERTAINMENT CABINET

This was another cabinet in my coach with no shelving; as a result all the remotes and the radio would be piled in on top of the home theater and be difficult to find when they were required.

The solution was a simple shelf constructed from ¼ inch plywood with paint sticks as trim. The right side of the shelf had to float to accommodate all the home theater hardware. This is shown in the pictures.

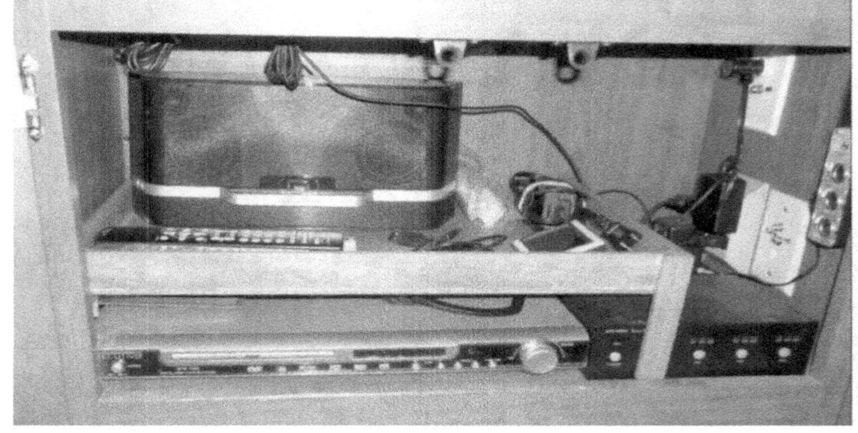

RECLAIM SPACE

In our RV bedroom we have mounted a flat panel TV. I often wondered what was behind it so one day I took the TV down and found a large unfinished space. Using some ¼ inch plywood I finished the side walls and bottom of this space, I added a shelve and put a hinge on one side of the TV frame and fasteners on the other. The TV is now the door for the new space.

I use this reclaimed space as my office supply cupboard. It is also a perfect space for my printer, copier, and scanner combination unit as electricity was already there for the TV.

Cost to accomplish this modification, $30.00

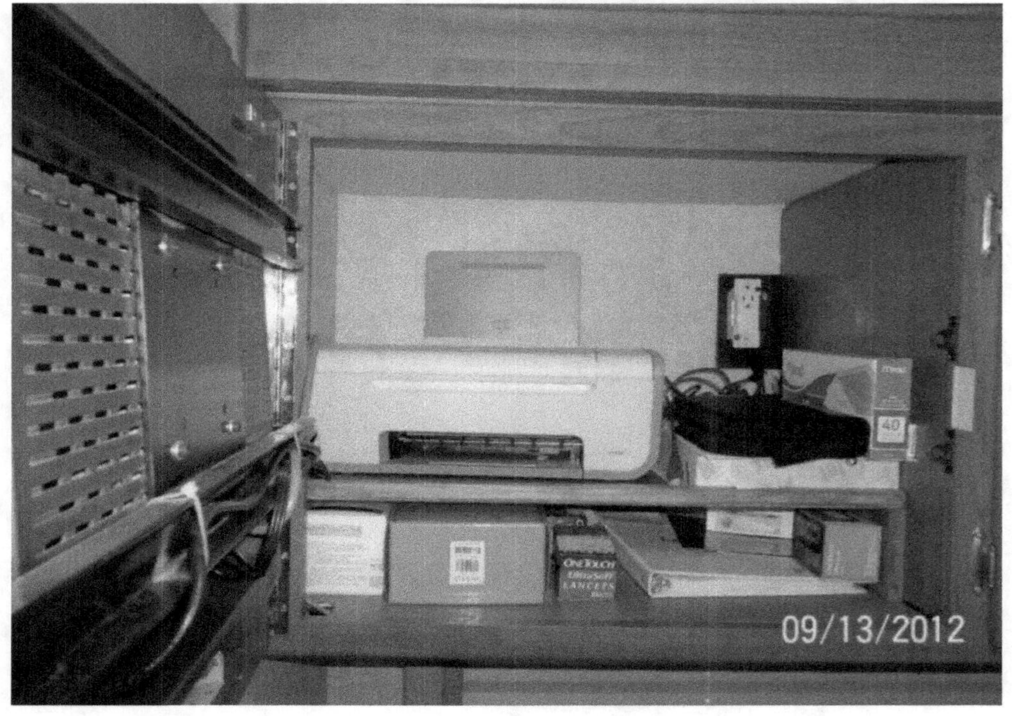

An item that is always missing in an RV is towel rods. No matter who the manufacture is they always seem to omit them. Why? Is it lack of wall space or perhaps how to you attach them to the thin walls?

I found space in my RV on the back of the bathroom door. I selected rods that matched the decor and other hardware in the bathroom and attached per instructions.

I took a page from the solar industry and attached the towel rods using "well nuts". They can hold almost anything on the thinnest walls. Well nuts can be found in the specialty section of the large box stores. Below is a graphic showing how they work.

To use well nuts you drill a hole large enough for the rubber of the nut to fit through. Insert the nut into the hole and with a bolt about ¼ inch longer than the rubber attach the towel bracket to the door face. The well nut will compress in the hole holding the bracket secure. Then attach the rod to the bracket.

Below is a nice graphic of how well nuts work.

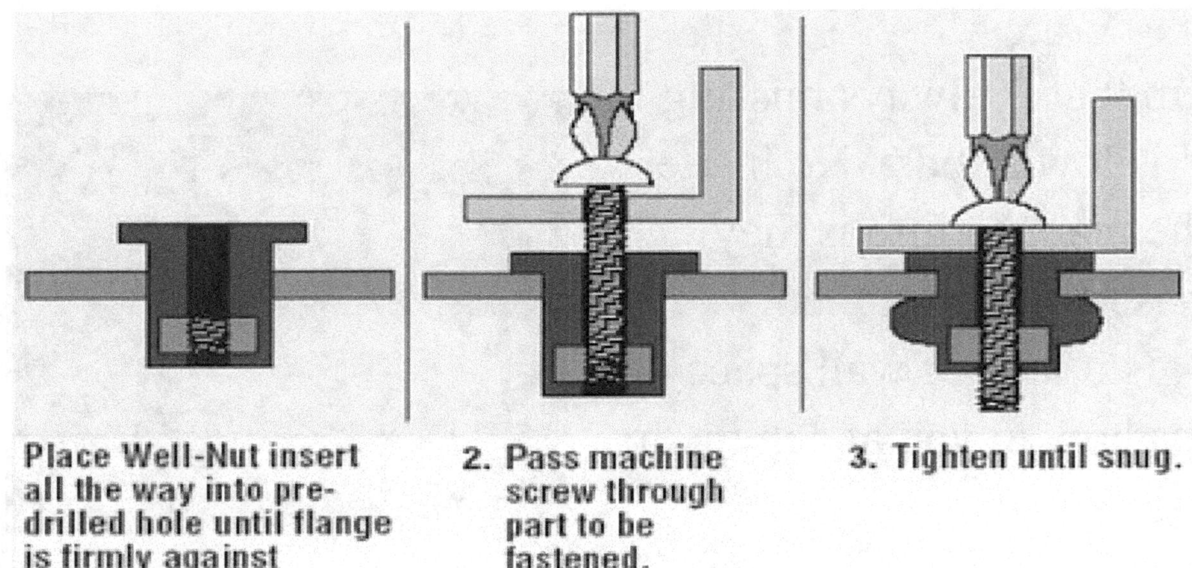

Do you travel with your fur babies? We do and I am always concerned for their and our safety. What is there is an accident and they go flying? What if I need to get to the brake and one in under foot? There would be an accident for sure. For these reasons we always travel with the babies crates. Fortunately they were crate trained when young and they consider the crate a safe haven.

Recently I say this modification that I thought was fantastic. This gentleman has a bunkhouse motorhome. As he did not need the bunks for sleeping he uses the top for storage and the bottom as a pet condo. This is accomplished by purchasing a outdoor pet play yard. These are normally made up of sections and set up in a hexagon or octagon depending on the size you get. There is always a door in one section that can be hocked shut.

What this gentleman did was to take several sections of the play yard as well as the gate section and attach them to the lower and upper bunk. He had an instant pet condo that the fur baby appears to love. Makes me wish I had a bunk house motorhome.

Another less expensive solution might be to purchase a children's play gate and install so that it can be pulled across the lower bunk.   I will caution that with the play gate approach make sure the gate cannot be pushed out by your pet at the middle bottom of the gate.   You know how mischievous your fur baby can be. I can imagine mine escaping and trotting to the front of the coach and jumping on the dash with that daddy aren't I cute smile.

REMOTE LIGHT SWITCH

This is something for shall we say the height challenged among us. How many have ceiling lights and or ceiling fans in their RVs and no wall switches by which to turn them on? So many manufacturers use the switches on the device which is on the ceiling and the only way to reach them is ether have a tall spouse turn things on or use a stool. Another solution, install a remote control device.

The first one I want to discuss is strictly for LED lighting applications. Not only will it allow the remote turn on/off of the light but it also provides for dimming of the light. The main module is the size of a pack of cigarettes and can be mounted next to the light or in the ceiling above the light. Simply

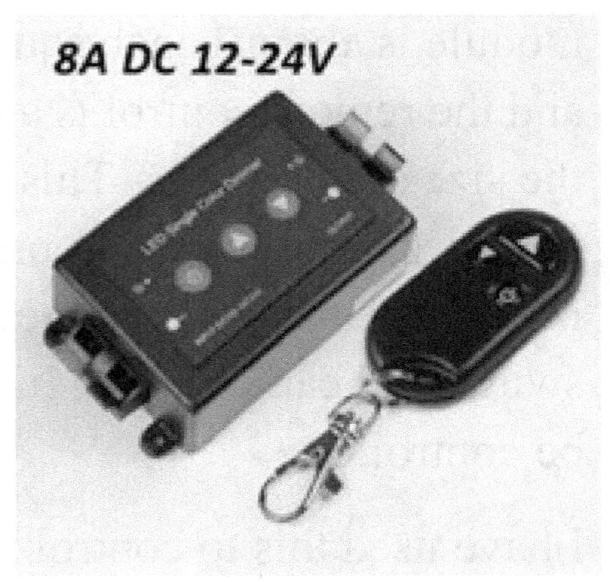

cut the wires to the light and attach them to the control module input then the device to be controlled to the control module output. The installation is complete. The remote control is the size of a key fob.

This device may be obtained at the provided web address. I have installed this and it works great.

http://www.banggood.com/8A-DC12-24V-LED-Strip-Light-Single-Color-Dimmer-Controller-With-Wireless-R emote-p-987970.html

This second device can be used for LED lighting, incandescent lighting or fans. It is a remote control relay module. The main module is about 1 inch square and the remote control is again the size of a key fob. This device provides on/off function only. It installs the same as the previous switch and can easily be hidden under the light, fan or device to be controlled.

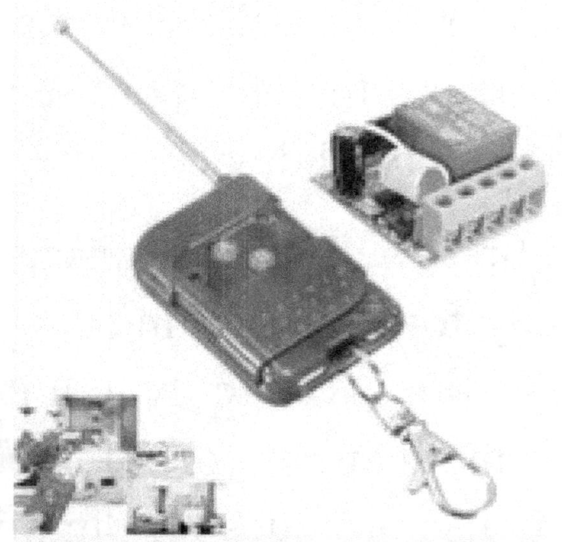

I have used this to control an 18 inch ceiling fan that I installed over the dining table of my RV. This device can be obtained at the following web address. (Please note the relay module did come enclosed in a black plastic box on the one I received.)

https://www.banggood.com/DC-12V-10A-1CH-433MHz-Relay-Wireless-RF-Remote-Control-Switch-Receiver-With-Transmitter-p-1101046.html?rmmds=search

Here is a real nice remote switch that a friend brought to my attention. Like the others it is installed in the hot line of the light, may be hidden behind the light, then you simply leave the light on and use the new switch. I may put these in the bedroom not because I cannot reach the light switch but because I cannot reach it while in bet.

The switch can be purchased with from one to three receivers allowing you to control multiple lights. If interested search the internet for "12 Volt wireless on off remote control transmitter with receiver switch"

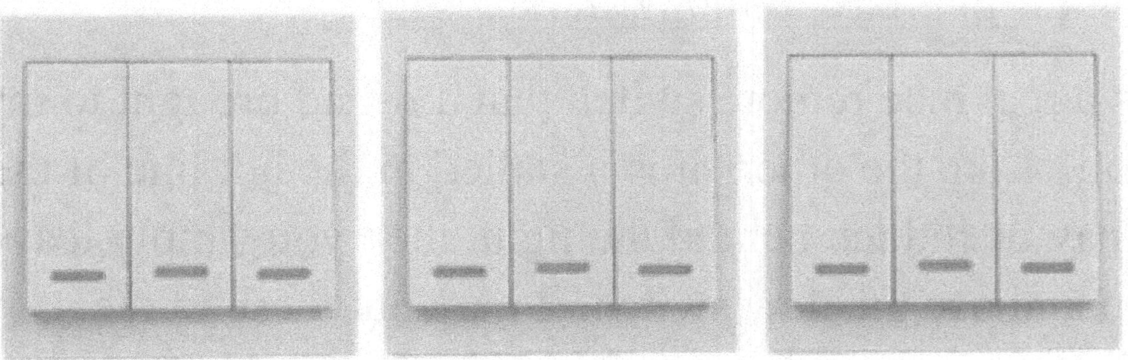

The maximum price I have seen for this item is $35.00 for the three switch set.

FAN-TASTIC-VENT FAN REVERSE

During those nice hot sticky summer days known as the dog days of summer, wouldn't it be nice if you could cool the old RV a little more easily, or provide a breath of fresh air? Perhaps with this modification you can. I believe every RV has at least one ceiling vented fan and many have two or more. Most of these fans are set to exhaust the air. What if you could have one set to exhaust and one set to intake? This would create a nice air flow through the RV. Given these fans are nothing more than DC motors all you need to do to get them to run in reverse is to change the polarity of the power applied to the motor. This can easily be accomplished with a double pole double through switch wired as shown. The switch can be obtained from eBay. I have done this to two of my fans and it works great. All the information is provided.

2PCS 6Pin DPDT ON-OFF-ON 3 Position Snap Boat Rocker Switch AC 6A/250V 10A/125V

$0.99
Trending at $1.66
Buy It Now

From China

Top Rated Plus

View of fan with new switch
installed.

Detail wiring diagram.

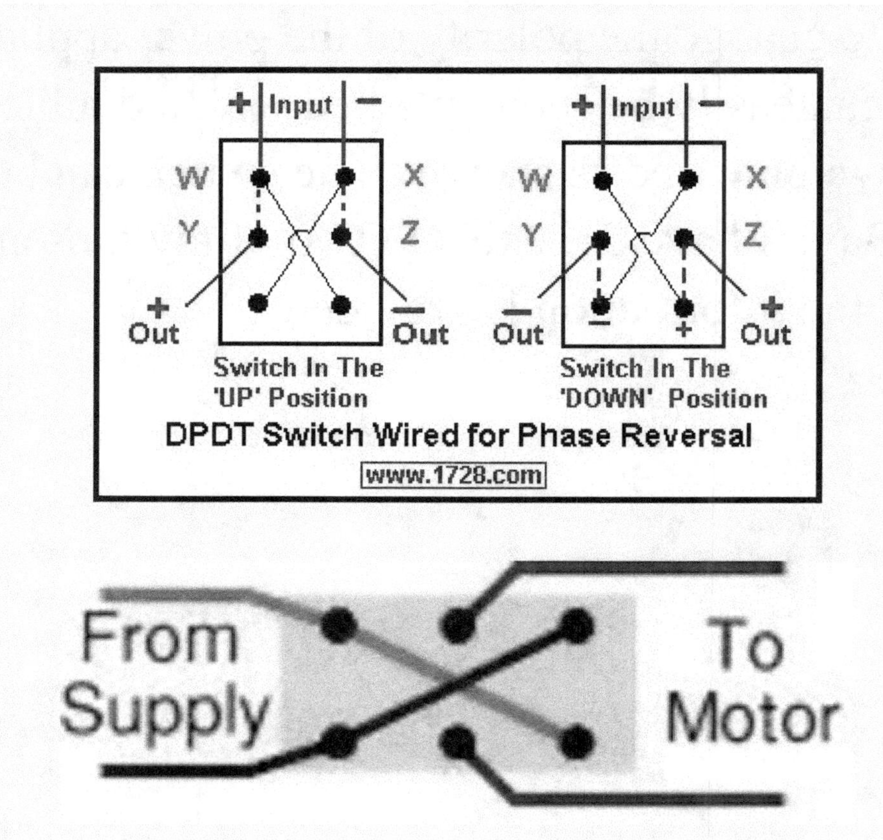

FAN-TASTIC-VENT POP 'N Lock Screen

If you have one of the older Fan-Tastic fans in your roof vent the fan screen is probably held in place by a dozen screws. This makes cleaning the screen difficult. You have to take out the screws to remove the screen. You usually drop several of these tiny things in the process. Then you get to crawl around on the floor looking for them so you can put the screen back. For less than a twenty dollar bill this problem is eliminated by the Pop'N Lock Screen. I have them and they are great. You can find them on Amazon or from an RV parts supplier.

The Pop'N Lock Screen

Will cover existing screw holes

Comes in colors to match your ceiling vent

Just snap on or off

FAN-TASTIC-VENT REMOTE UPGRADE

My wife is one of the height challenged people in this world so reaching the ceiling in our RV is not going to happen for her without the aid of a stool. This becomes a problem at shower time. I like to have the ceiling vent open and the fan running to pull the steam and moisture out of the RV. The wife however cannot reach the vent so I always get the "Honey" call. Searching on the internet I found a solution for this problem. For $150.00 to $200.00 Fan-Tastic Vent make an upgrade kit that replaces the inside trim for one that has the following features:

- Motorized vent door
- Rain sensor will close the vent during a storm
- A remote control that runs all fan operations
- Pop'N Lock Screen
- Reverse switch

The kit comes with detailed instructions for a DIY project. Installation can be done in less than an hour.

View of parts in the Vent kit.

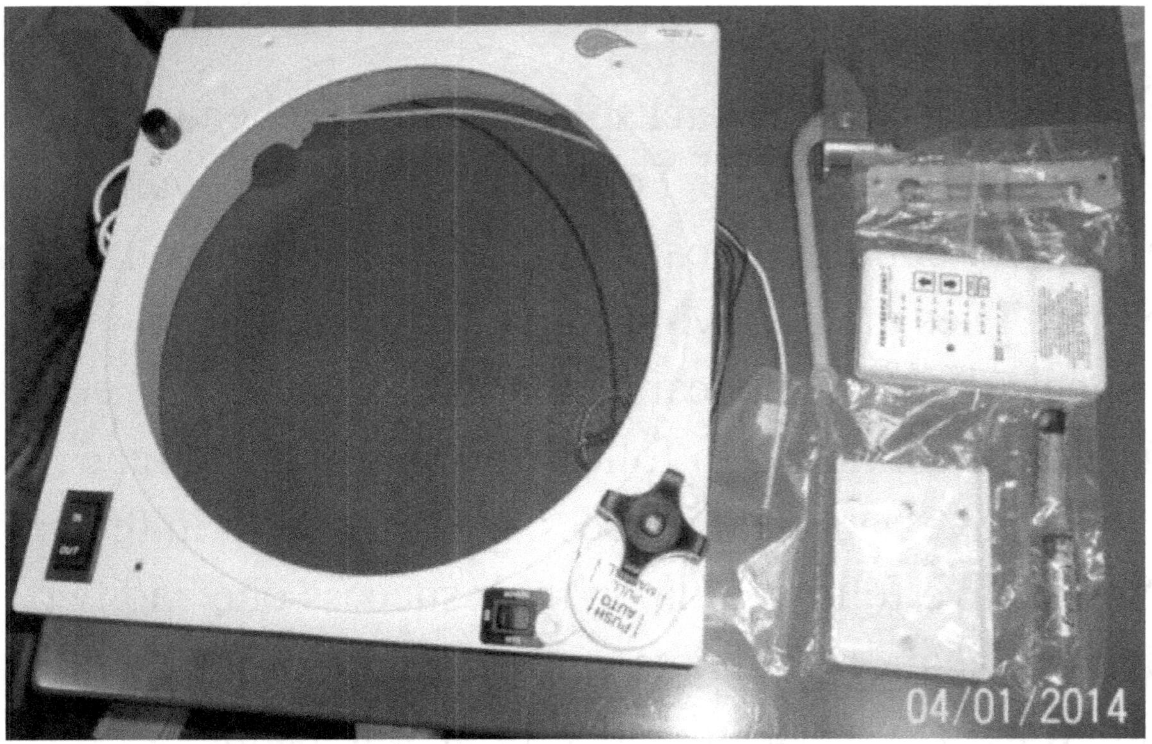

View of the completed install and the new Remote.

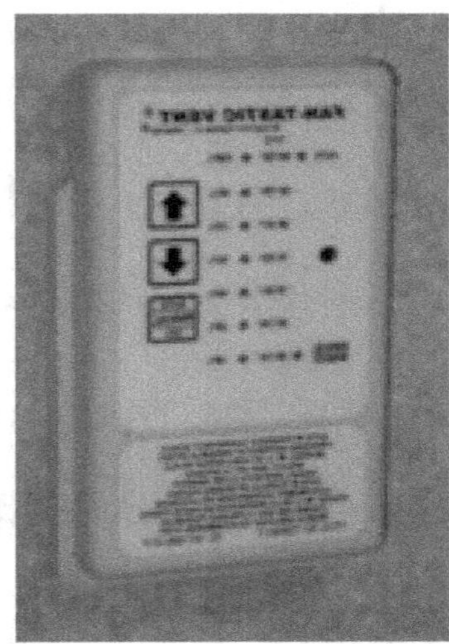

Having an older coach the backsplash in the kitchen area was finished with just wallpaper. For some time I have wanted to dress this up. A couple of years ago I read an article on Smart Tiles. Smart Tiles are a vinyl product that comes in 10 inch by 10 inch sheets, have the appearance of tile, and have an epoxy backing. I have continued to follow this product and read where others have had great success applying them in their RV's. Some have followed up on their success one and two years after application and have confirmed the product still looks like new. This year I decided to give it a shot.

While Smart Tile is a brand name for the product which can be purchased through stores like Amazon, Lowes, and Homedepot there are other brands that come up if you do a Smart Tile search. I chose to go with Tic-Tac-Tiles because they had the pattern and color scheme I preferred.

Preparation for the installation involved removal of any loose wallpaper on the backsplash and then a thorough cleaning with a degreasing agent.

Tools needed were a razor knife, scissors, straight edge, cutting board, and measure. From collecting the tools to applying the tiles and cleaning up only took three hours. I finished the edges with ½ inch chair rail stained maple to match the coach. I was so pleased with the results I even did the backsplash of the two vanities. My cost was $80.00

Unless you actually touch the product you cannot tell it is not real tile and even then you can be fooled. They are anti mold/mildew treated, water proof, and only added ten pounds to the weight of the RV. See pictures below of before, during, and the completed job.

Tiles can be cut with Knife or Scissors

Completed

I was so pleased with the kitchen area I used the left over and scrap tiles and did the back of the two bathroom vanities.

Before Center Vanity

Completed Center Vanity

Completed Bath Room Vanity

HANDRAIL

While at the factory for a tour I noticed that the new model coaches had two handrails by the doors, one on each side. On my return home I checked the RV supply store and found the same handrail the factory was using. For $21.00 and the cost of four screws I too had a second handrail.

WASHER DRYER

This one I cannot take credit for. Right after I purchased my coach I wanted it outfitted with a washer / dryer. Not knowing how I would get it into the coach I went back to the factory. There I purchased the washer / dryer option and had them install it. It turned out that the unit just fit through the door. The plumbing, vent, and electric were already in place as my coach had the washer dryer prep package.

If you do not have electricity wouldn't it be nice if you could still charge cell phones, tablets, and computers? You do have

the RV battery as a power source you just need the charging stations. If you check eBay or Amazon you can find many 12 Volt DC outlets and USB charging stations for as little as $5.00 each. I mounted mine in two locations in my coach and tied them into the electric for the adjacent lights.

Charging station installed next to light switch. Power was tapped from the switch.

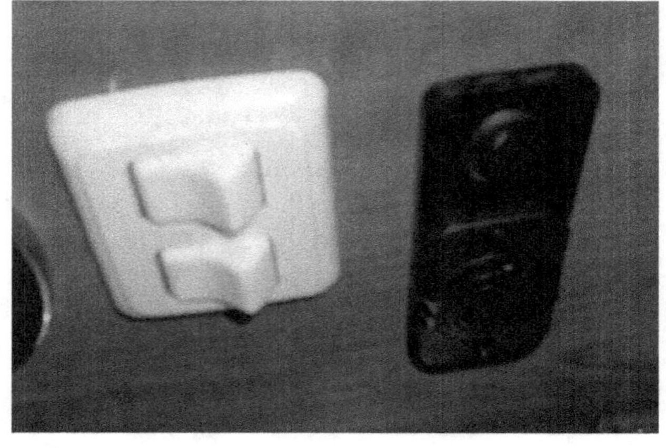

CLOCK AND WEATHER STATION

This is an extremely useful modification and simple to accomplish.

New clock has weather station with outside transmitter sensor. I mounted the Temperature on my slide rail out of the sun.

SCREEN DOOR CROSS BAR

This is a simple modification that will protect the screen door and can be installed in less than 15 minutes. Cost about $10.00 depending where you find it.

Available at most RV supply stores or on line it comes in white or black and is adjustable to fit the door width.

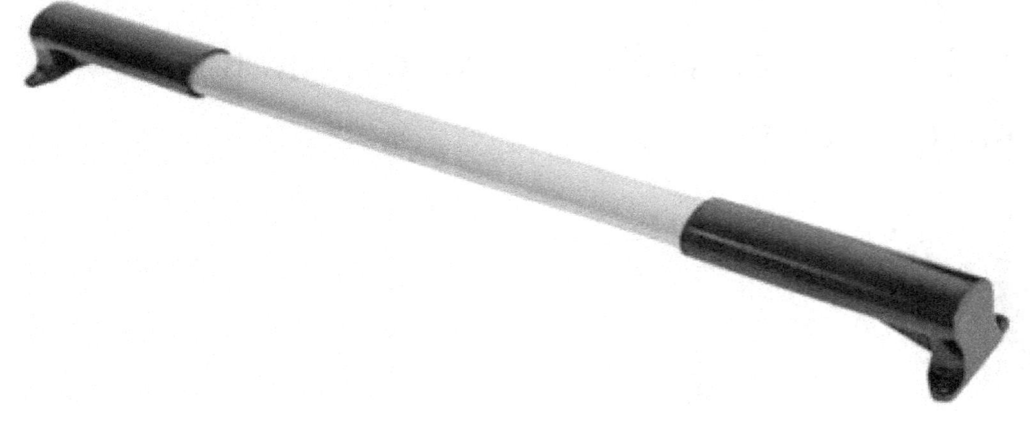

UPGRADE RADIO SPEAKER

My current motorhome came with two inch speakers for the dash radio. When stopped they did not sound bad but when in motion they could not be driven above the road noise. My solution was to purchase a pair of "Boss MR652C Marine 6.5" 350 Watt Stereo Speakers" from Amazon open box. Cost was only $25.60.

Using a six inch hole saw, I made a hole right next to the two inch speaker and simply moved the wires over to the new speakers. What a difference.

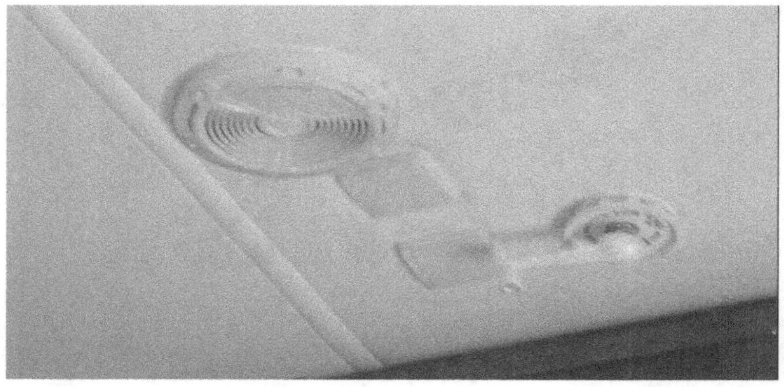

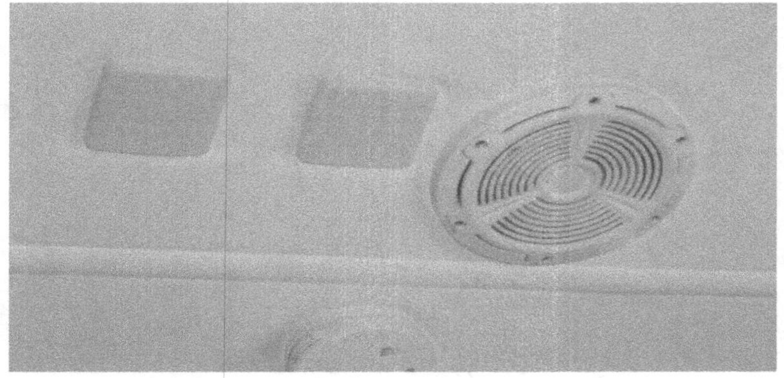

PIN SWITCHES

Many of us have lights in the compartments of our RVs but for one reason or another never use them. Often the light is in an inconvenient location or the slide out is over the compartment and one would need the arms of a gorilla to reach the light switch to turn it on. A solution I have found to this problem is to install pin switches on the compartment door frame. These switches will turn the light on automatically when the door is opened and off when closed. The way this works is that the light is left on. The pin switch is connected to the negative side of the light wiring. Whenever the door is open the switch will connect the wire and complete the circuit turning the light on. The light wiring can be accessed by taking the light down from where it is mounted. Snip the ground wire then add a new length of from the cut point to the location you choose for the pin switch. Reinstall the light and connect to the pin switch and you are finished. When choosing which of the two wires going to the light to route to the switch I choose the ground or negative side. The negative side is attached to the pin switch because often the switch will be connected to the chassis frame which is battery ground. In this case if you attached the positive light wire it would result in a short and blow the circuit fuse.

.

There are two style doors often found on an RV. One has a frame as shown above. For this style of door I recommend the switch below.

https://www.amazon.com/Pactrade-Marine-Security-Adjustable-Switch/dp/B01JASKG24/ref=sr_1_39?ie=UTF8&qid=1492048403&sr=8-39&keywords=pin+switch

The second style door has a flush frame. As depicted in the picture below.

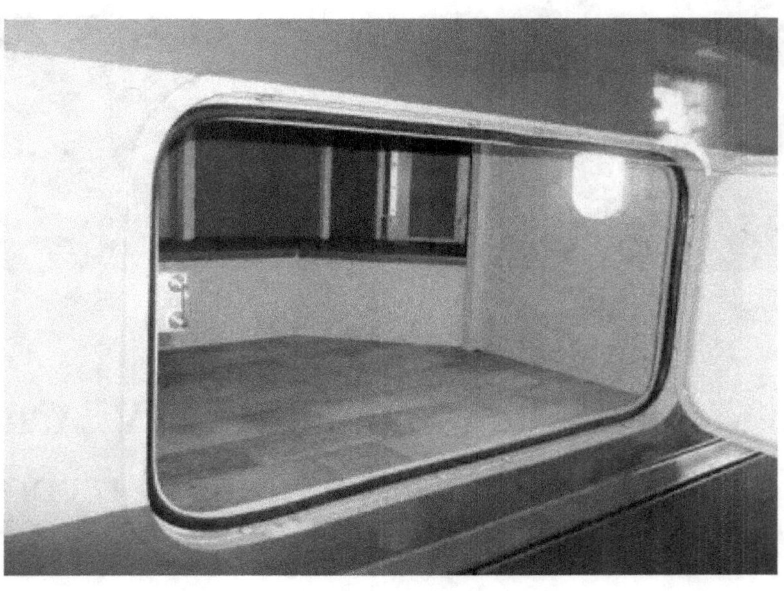

For this style door I recommend the following switch be used

https://www.amazon.com/Nickel-Plated-Switch-Polycarb-Plunger/dp/B001TQWOOO/ref=pd_sim_107_5?_encoding=UTF8&pd_rd_i=B001TQWOOO&pd_rd_r=FHZPZA32DCVABBME3KM0&pd_rd_w=biuWk&pd_rd_wg=kwmrE&psc=1&refRID=FHZPZA32DCVABBME3KM0

Most motorhomes have a mud flap the entire length of the coach. If you have to be towed the mud flap will either have to be removed or tied up. One way to make this a non issue is to put eyes in the mud flap. You can then hock a bungee cord and secure the mud flap up and out of the way using the coach trailer hitch.

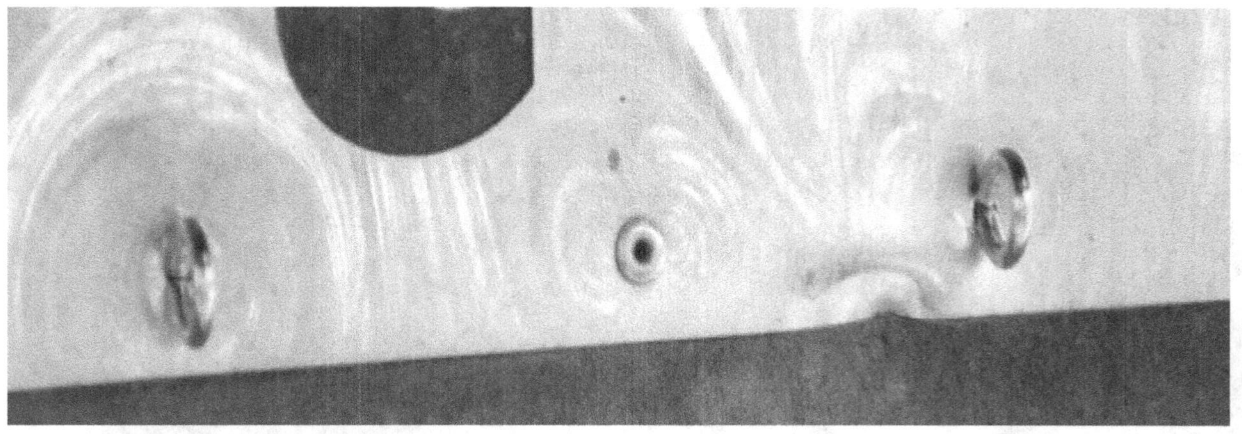

I have mentioned before that my coach is very low to the ground. If not careful the backend will drag on hills and when going out parking lots with culverts. To help to protect the coach I installed skid wheels on the back. Yes they work. Easy bolt on and sold at many RV parts stores. They are purchased per the weight of your application or coach. Mine cost $57.00.

FRONT MUD FLAPS

What do they say, get that first scratch on a new vehicle over with? That happened to me with my brand new motorhome back in 2008. Not over 100 miles from the dealer on my way home debris left on the road by a work crew got kicked up by my front tire and put a 4 foot dent and scrape on the bottom of my basement door. Once home I pounded out the dent, painted the door and then added mud flaps to the front tire wells. Very simple, I went to the local auto store and picked up the big truck style rubber mud flaps, screwed them on and used a piece of metal as stiffener along the flap. The install picture clearly shows the metal stiffener.

BASEMENT STORAGE

Fifth wheels, motorhomes and some travel trailers have deep and tall basement storage compartments. You load them up with everything you need and when you get to camp the item you want is always on the bottom of the pile. Now you have to dig to get it. A real pain.

I solved this problem by building a shelf in the basement of my motorhome. I designed it just the right height to allow under bed sweater boxes to slide in. The RV is just wide enough to accommodate two boxes back to back. Great for tools, small part organization and sewer hose storage. Chairs and big items go on top. You can find them almost anywhere. My upgrade, shelf and six boxes cost $100.00.

ACCUMULATOR TANK

Want to give your water pump a break? Install an accumulator tank. The tank will take noise out of the system, relieve pressure on the hot water tank, and give the pump a break by letting it rest longer between on/off cycles.

This picture shows the install of a SHURFLO Accumulator Tank Model 182. It simply screwed in on the output side of the pump.

WINTERIZING PUMP SWITCH

A popular way to winterize an RV is to pump pink through the water lines using the on board water pump. My pump is in an outside compartment but the water pump switch is inside the coach. I am constantly yelling for the wife to turn off the pump as I change to a fresh gallon of pink. I made the whole process easier by adding a switch out at the pump that interrupts power. Now when winterizing I turn the pump on in inside and can turn it off and on after that right at the pump.

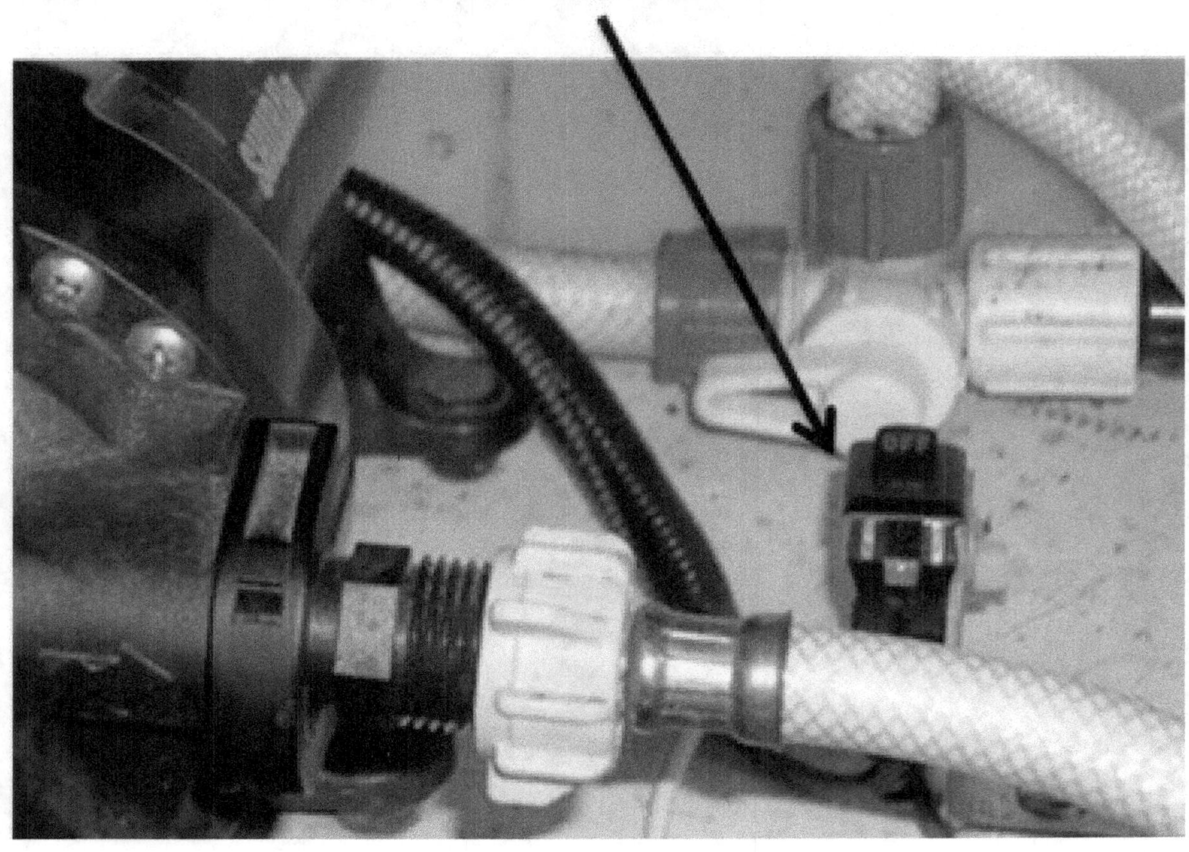

RV PROPANE TANK COVER MODIFICATION TO CHECK FILL

Even as RV design continues to improve and adapt, there still seems to be small lapses in design where you wonder "Why don't they do it this way?". One such head scratcher is the propane tank and cover. It commonly appears on the front of travel trailers, tends to be white in color, and I have yet to see one that allows you to see inside at the tanks. In order to check how much propane is left you have to remove the cover, remove the tank and feel its weight.

This modification is the perfect solution to this problem. It is quite simple to do and should not take more than a few minutes to complete.

The modification requires just a small piece of acrylic-glass, some pop rivets, and a propane level gauge for each tank.

To do this modification, install the level gauges. Using a hole saw create a strategically placed hole in the tank cover that will allow you to see the gauges. Then simply cut the acrylic-glass to the right size to seal off the hole and pop rivet or screw it into place.

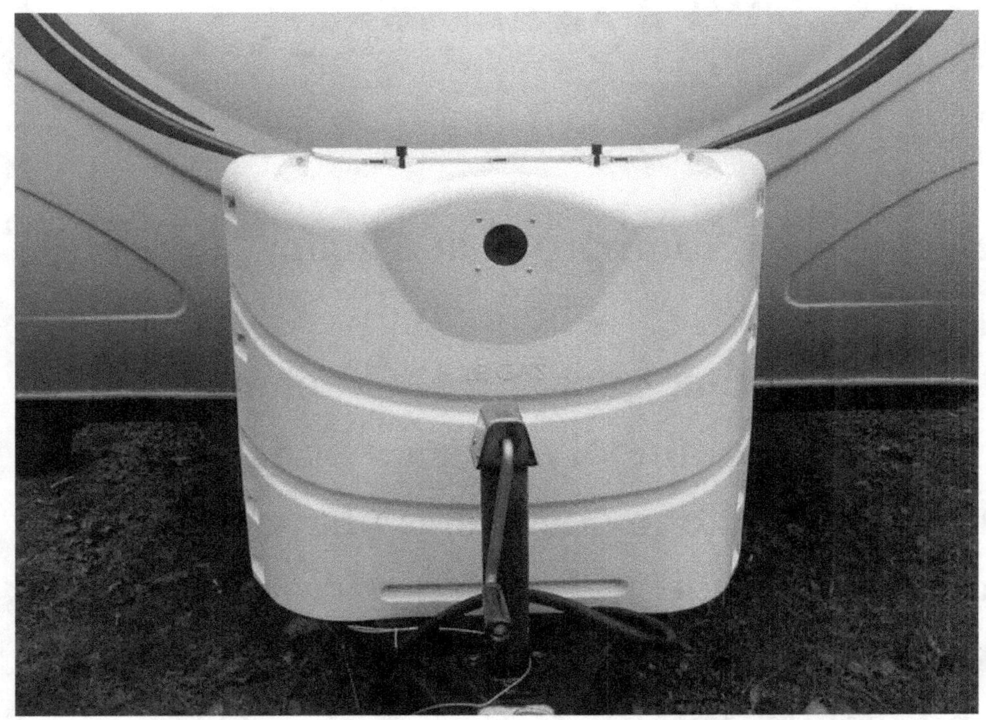

With any luck and the right positioning, you should be staring through your propane tank cover and see how much or how little propane you have left for the rest of the trip.

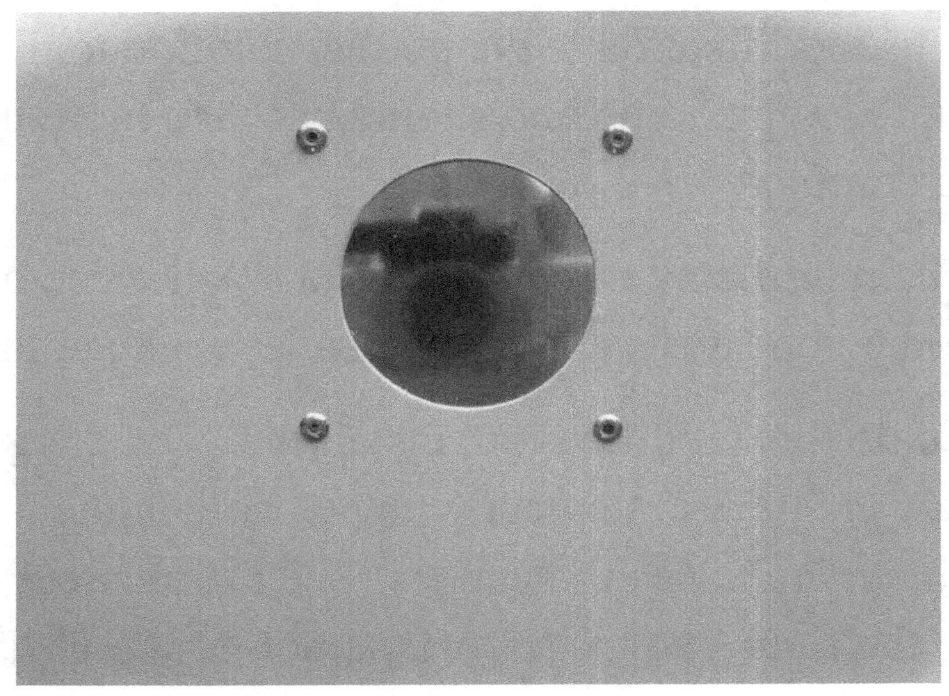

TRICK TO AVOID REPLACING FAILING GAS SPRINGS

My coach turns 10 years old this year. The RV manufacture made liberal use of gas springs on all the basement storage doors. For the doors that open sideways there is not much of an issue but for the doors that open up when the springs fail you ether use your head to hold the door open or have to replace the springs. There is an alternative. Use PVC pipe to support the spring.

Over time (sometimes not long at all) the combination of the high pressure inside these springs and the fact that they're almost always in a closed state putting a lot of stress on the seals. It's just a matter time before the springs fail.

Cut a few pieces of 1 inch (depends on diameter of the spring) PVC to length and rip a 1/4″ slot down the middle, make it wide enough to slip over the extended arm of the gas spring. The PVC pipe slips over the arm and wedges between the door and the top of the gas spring housing. When you're ready to close the hatch, you just slide the pipe down and shut the door. The PVC support will remain attached to

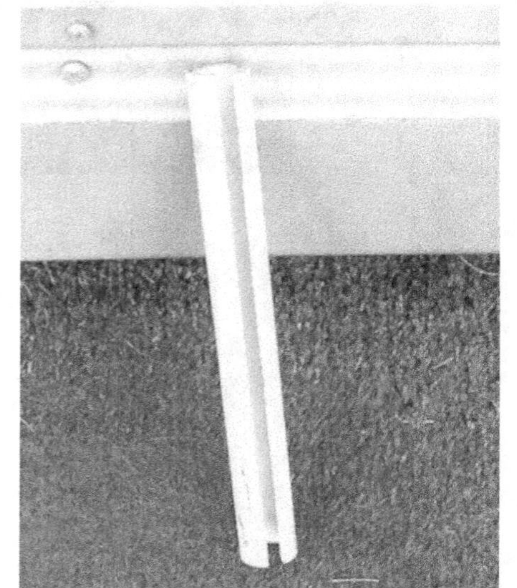

the spring, and safely out of the way, allowing the door to close flush.

Depending on the girth of your RV gas springs, the PVC support may not slide over the housing easily. Others have struggled with this and decided to simply lay the PVC pipe directly inside the storage bay for easy access. When you want the PVC pipe to hold the door up, just slip it into position.

MAXX AIR VENT COVER

I have had MaxxAir vent covers on my RVs since the early 2000s. They allow you to have the vent open in the rain or during other bad weather conditions. Some are even equipped with fans that aid circulation.

The biggest benefit of a MaxxAir cover in my opinion is you can leave a vent open 24/7. This keeps the RV from overheating in the summer and helps moisture escape in winter.

From the picture above you can see I have two styles of covers over my vents. The one on the right I do not believe is made any longer. The one on the left I feel is better as it affords all the protection needed and lets the RV vent open further for better air flow.

A misperception regarding roof vent covers is that you have to drill holes in the roof of the RV to attach them. This is not true. The brackets holding the vents are attached to the side of the roof vent. Tools needed are an electric drill and a couple of wrenches or rivet gun. To follow are detail pictures of an install I did. The first is a close up of the installed bracket and second the vent cover installed. Cost of a vent cover can run $30.00 to $50.00 depending where you shop.

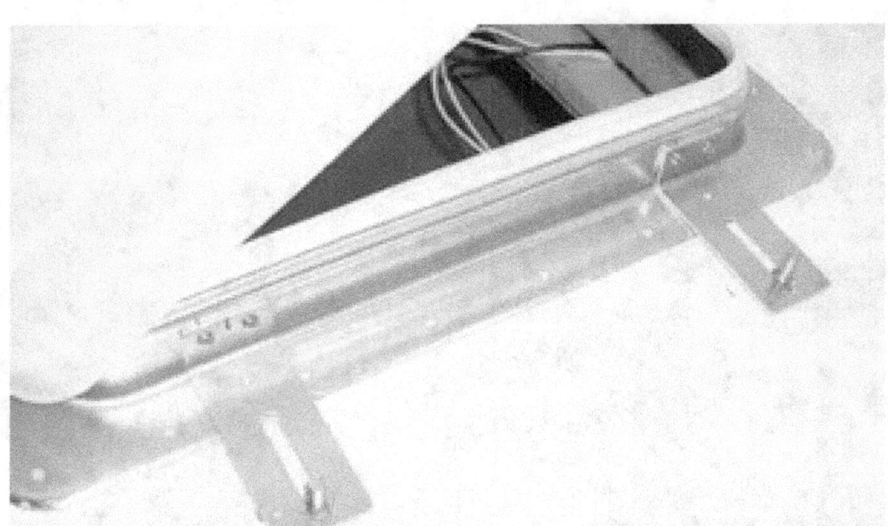

The newer style cover shown left hinge open. These are much nicer than the old bolt to bracket style. Makes cleaning so much easier.

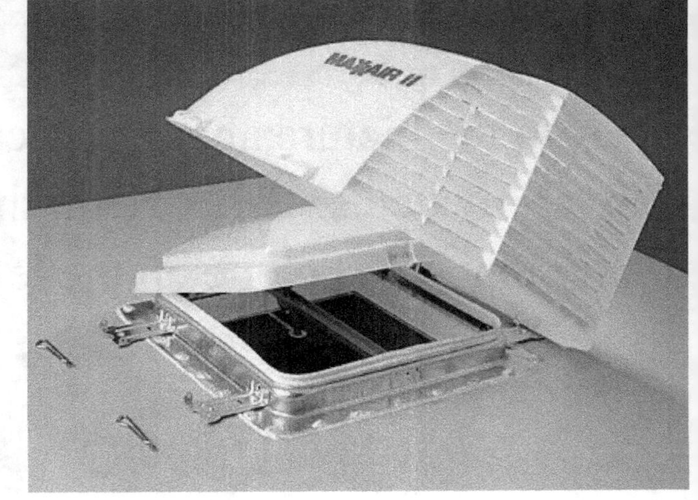

Do you have a motorhome and often run out of propane? Want to get more without packing up and pulling the coach out?

Would you like to connect your propane grill into the RV gas system?

One way to accomplish both these things is with an extend-a-stay device. Easily installed between the RV and the regulator. I purchased the complete kit with hoses valve. It is Great.

HATCH LIFT

Do you have a basement door that came without a lift kit. There is a aftermarket product called Hatch Lift that may solve your problem. Hatch Lift comes in different sizes and strengths. It comes with everything you need to install a gas filled spring on any door. I purchased two of their largest kits for my water bay door. The cost was around $70.00.

FREEZE PREVENTION FOR WET BAY

During early spring and late fall camping I am always worried about frost and freezing of the lines in my water bay. I could leave the heat running in the RV but that uses a lot of energy. On cold nights my dad would take his trouble light out to the RV, turn it on, and put in the cupboard with the water lines. It provided just enough heat to prevent freezing. I did this for several years but got tired of having to drag the light out and put it in place. My solution was to install sockets for lights into the wet bay. You just have to remember only the old incandescent light throw off heat. I found 60 watt bulbs worked for me. To follow is the parts list and pictures.

2 x LightCage Light Bulb Safty Cage	$19.00
2 x Three Inch Ceiling Box	$4.20
2 x Ceiling Lamp Holder	$2.52
2 x PVC block 4"x4"x1/2"	$0.00
2 x 60 watt Light Bulb	$0.00
14ag Three Wire Extension Cord	$0.00
Heat Shield Material	$0.00
total	$25.72

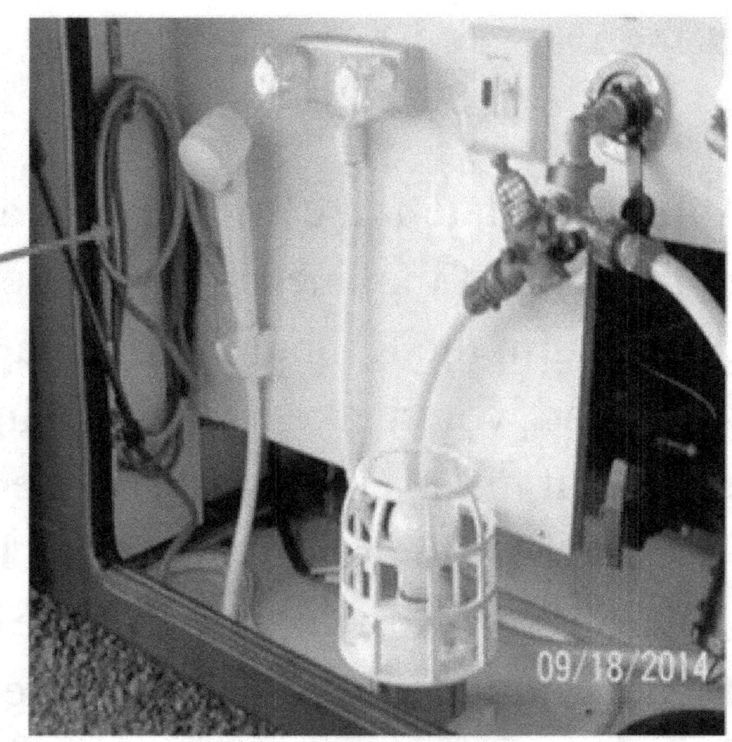

Cord to be
plugged
into
pedestal
or block
heater
plug in
power bay

09/18/2014

Fashioned heat shield to protect
Fresh and gray water tanks but do
Not believe it is necessary.   Better
Safe than sorry.

I love the little LED flashlights. I find them small enough to fit in my pocket and very powerful. In addition to the flashlights I have accumulated many remotes to run all the toys I have installed. Where do these things end up? The famous JUNK drawer that we all have then when I needed one of them I have to paw through the drawer. I had to find a better solution. I found on eBay a "Car Seat Side Storage Net Pocket Organizer BC4U" and a soap dish. These items I mounted on the dash of the motorhome and by the main entry door. Now the remotes and flashlights are stored where they are used. Cost was $2.00 per each item.

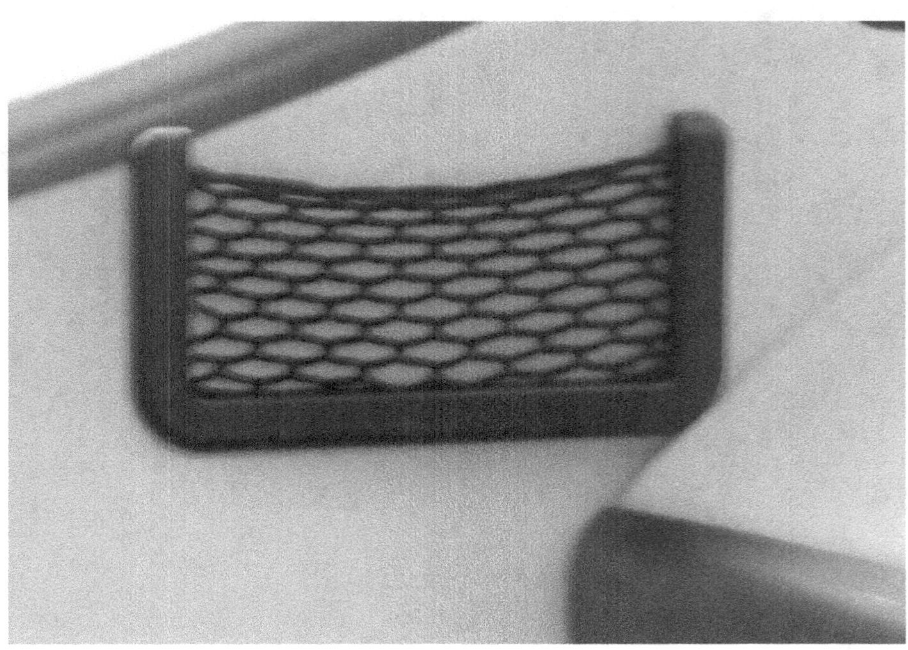

LED Remote Controller

FRESH WATER Y & GRAY TANK FLUSH

This past spring I made a couple of enhancements in my water bay. The first was to install a Tornado Flush in my gray water tank. The second was to install a water pleasure regulator and Y system that allows me to easily switch my fresh water hose from the city inlet to tank fill and my flush hose from gray tank flush to black tank flush. While not necessary, like many enhancements they just make things a little more convenient. To follow are pictures and parts list.

Camco 40126 Tornado Rotary Tank Rinser with Hose	$24.98
90 Degree Hose Connector Elbow RV Water Faucet Camco	$23.84
AHP 2-Way Garden Hose Connector Y Valve Splitter	$17.90
RV white CITY WATER FILL inlet flange BRASS w/ check valve	$9.95
Random pieces of hose, on hand	$0.00
Total	$76.67

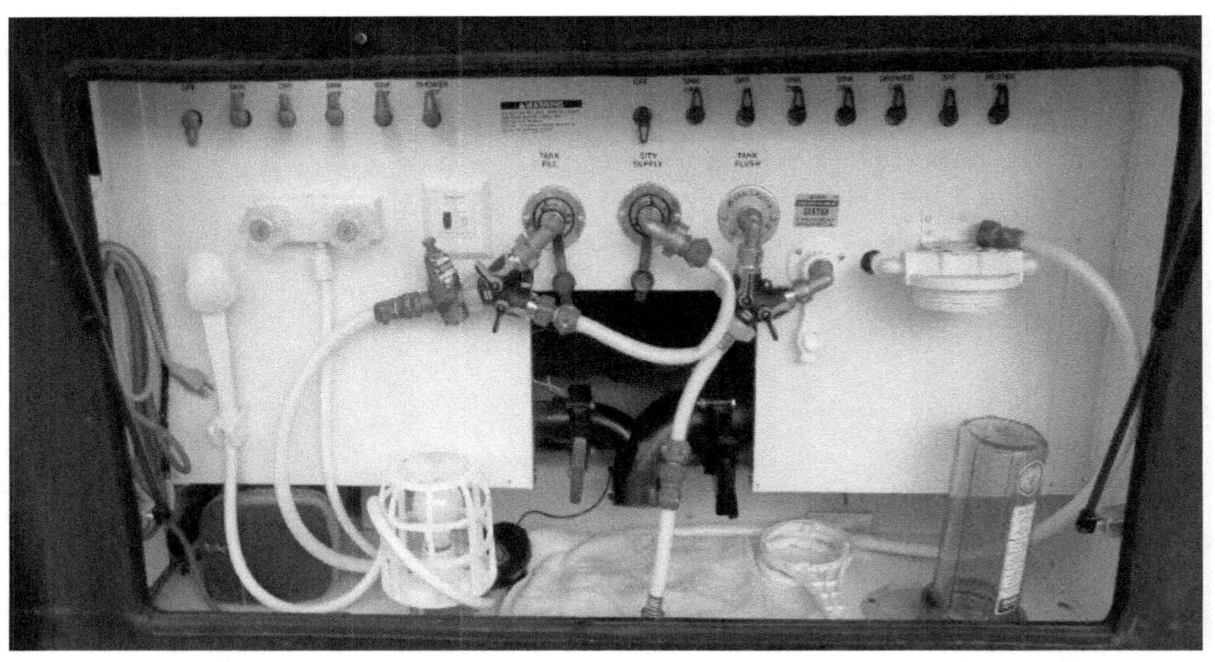

TRUCK BED ARMOR ON MOTORHOME

Every year during my spring detailing I would spend a day going around the motorhome and touching up all the little rock chips that has accrued the previous year. The majority of the chips were located on the bottom of the basement doors. I thought there should be some cost effective way to protect this area. I did my research and found stainless steel strips that could be purchased for a small fortune but remember I want Cost effective. I finally got around to truck Bed Armor. I chose to use "Dupli-color Bed Armor Spray" for $12.00 each bottle. I prepared the surface by masking off the coach, scuffing the area to be treated, and cleaning with acetone. I sprayed three coats and the results were beautiful. Looks like a factory option. I did this along the entire length of the coach.

One of the three types of slides on my coach works on a rack and pinion system. The motor that drives this weighs about fifteen pounds and is about one foot long. The gear box on this motor has a pot metal housing. If you are familiar with pot metal it is not very strong. The motor and gear assembly are connected to the rack and pinion by four bolts through the pot metal. The biggest problem with this type of slide is that due to road vibrations and the weight of the motor it continues to slip down making the slide not work. When you tighten the bolts to try and secure the motor the pot metal housing will crack as it did with me.

Solution I came up with was to repair the gear box with JB-Weld. I then made a wedge support which I placed under the motor. This has been in place and worked well for the past five years.

08/1

08/19/2014

Many people complain that their black tank and gray tank gauges are not accurate. This is normally due to debris build up on the probes. A product that uses external tank gauges and will not have this problem is called SeeLevel. I purchased their model 709 which has sensors for fresh water, gray water, and black water tanks and also a sensor for the propane tank. The SeeLevel system is designed such that they can use existing OEM wiring or you can run new wires. I choose to run new wires and mount my sensors on the opposite side of the tanks from the original OEM sensors. This way I have two tank monitors working on each tank.

Attaching the sensors to the tanks was straight forward. Clean the surface of the tank, trim to fit per the instructions and apply to tank with the sticky tape provided.

Most RV manufactures bring their wires to one location and run them all together. It was very easy to find this location and snake m wires along with the coach builder's wires. This allowed me to put the SeeLevel control panel right next to my other coach controls.

The last thing to accomplish was to determine the connections for the propane monitor. Propane tanks have a restive float to determine the amount of fuel in them. The maximum resistance is 150 ohms and minimum resistance is zero. Using an ohm meter I located the lines that had this range of resistance on them and parallel these to the SeeLevel Propane tank monitor lines. I now had two fully working monitoring systems.

To follow are photos of the before, after, and during install. Total cost was $185.00.

Connections
And
Snaking
Tank Wires

New PVC
Tank Retainer
Prevent Interference

UNDER CABINET FAN

One way to stay cool is by moving the air. I won one of these several years back. It is designed to mount under the upper cabinets. It has two speeds, swivels, and folds up out of the way when not in use. A very simple and useful modification.

The name of the product is "Vornado V103 Under Cabinet Circulator" and can be purchased for around $40.00. If interested just search the internet for the name.

The bedroom in my RV has one window. On hot summer days there is not a breath of air in there and no cross ventilation. I thought how nice it would be to have a ceiling fan to keep the air moving at night.

About the time I was thinking about this some RV manufactures were beginning to install them but they used AC fans that ran either only when you had shore power connected or they ran them through a converter. These AC fans are large and heavy. I wanted to find a 12 volt DC fan that would run directly off the RV battery and had a remote control so that I did not have to run control wires. I found such a fan at http://www.rvstuff.com/ for $169.00 complete.

The next problem was installation. As most RVs have 12 volt power at every ceiling vent, including the air conditioner openings, finding power in the ceiling was not a problem. Routing could be however. I have found most RVs have rigid foam insulation in the ceiling or pink poly insulation. Routing through pink poly is fairly easy using an electrical snake. With a rigid foam ceiling I found a stiff electrical snake could push through the foam a fair distance without issue. When longer runs are necessary you can usually route to the air conditioning duct that then run the length of the RV then run the wiring through them.

To anchor the ceiling fan I took a page from the solar industry and used well nuts. They can hold almost anything to the thinnest materials. Well nuts can be found in the specialty section of the large box stores. Below is a graphic showing how they work.

To use well nuts you drill a hole large enough for the rubber of the nut to fit through. Insert the nut into the hole and with a bolt about ¼ inch longer than the rubber attach the bracket fan bracket to the ceiling. The well nut will compress in the hole holding the bracket secure.

Below is a nice graphic showing how well nuts work.

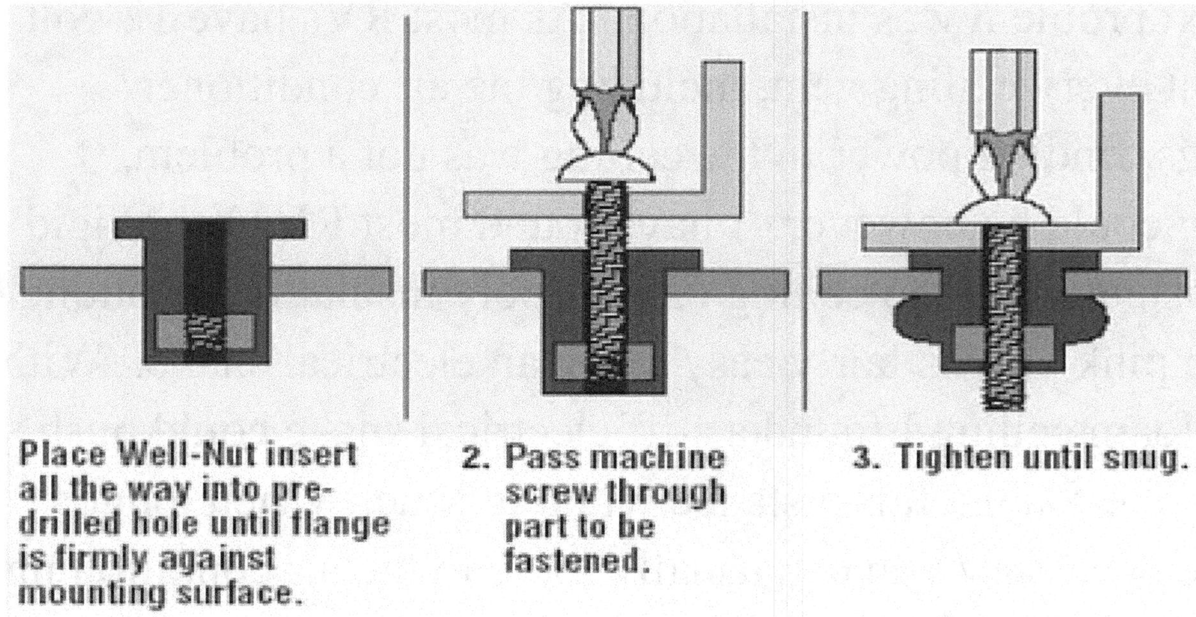

Having chosen a fan and solved the power and mounting problem it is time for the install.

When choosing the location to install the fan be sure it is clear of obstructions such as open cabinet doors and the slide walls when they are retracted. The picture shows the fan in the bedroom. As you can see it looks like it came with the RV.

This fan has been in my coach for eight years and has worked perfectly and never loosened despite 40,000 miles traveled. All the electronics are in the fan housing which is a plus. I have seen other 12 volt fans that require a junction box somewhere near them for the control electronics. This adds to the install complexity. Again the control is by IR remote the only connections are plus 12 volt and ground.

On occasion there will be a situation where the power wires cannot be routed in the ceiling. I ran into this situation in a tag axle coach. There I used conduit mounted to the ceiling with sticky tape to conceal the power wiring. I ran the conduit over to the air conditioning vent as we have discussed. Once in the vent I routed over to a ceiling vent and picked up power. Pictures of the install are above. Notice how good the conduit looks. It does not detract from the coach look at all.

This is where we picked up the 12 Volt supply at the ceiling fan vent.

The conduit was purchased from a big box store. It is self adhering and comes with all the pieces you will require. Price is $12.00 and is named "Mono-Systems, Inc. CordHider 9-Piece 144-in L White Raceway Kit"

The best way to keep an RV cool is to keep the heat out. On a motorhome one critical item needed to do this is the windshield shade. Back in 2011 MCD innovations (http://mcdinnovations.com) was gaining popularity as the primer shade provider for the motorhome industry. I read their web site which stated what information was needed to order a shade I gathered the information and gave them a call. Back then their windshield shades sold for $1200.00. They refused to sell to me. Their reason was no mere mortal could install one of their complex shades. REALLY! They referred me to an installer 500 miles away who told me not all coaches were suited to MCD products. I would need to travel the 500 miles, get my coach measured, return home while a shade was being made for my coach, and then travel back the 500 miles for the install. I DON''T THINK SO! So this mere mortal made his own electric shade for only $300.00 complete and installed.

Here are the components that make up my shade.

From eBay I got "8ft Remote Control Motorized Electric Roller Shade Rod DIY Kit". This is a 12 volt DC electric shade rod kit. I ran the electric wire down the passenger A pillar and under the dash to a 12 volt source. In my case the main awning switch.

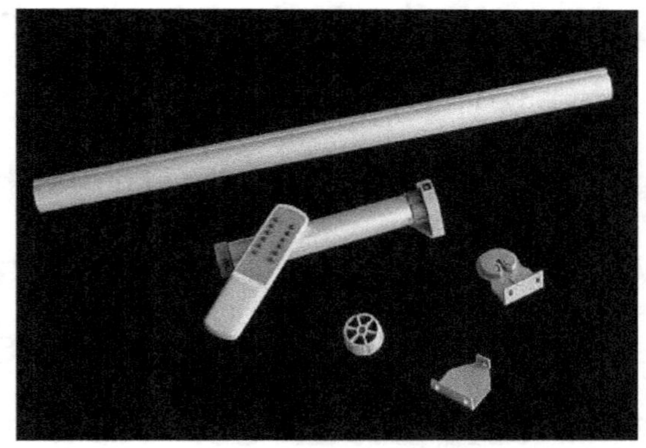

My wife went to the fabric store got material and sewed the shade. We covered a trim board with matching material and attached it all to the bottom side of the overhead cupboard above the windshield. See the photo for the result. Not bad for a mere mortal if I say so myself!

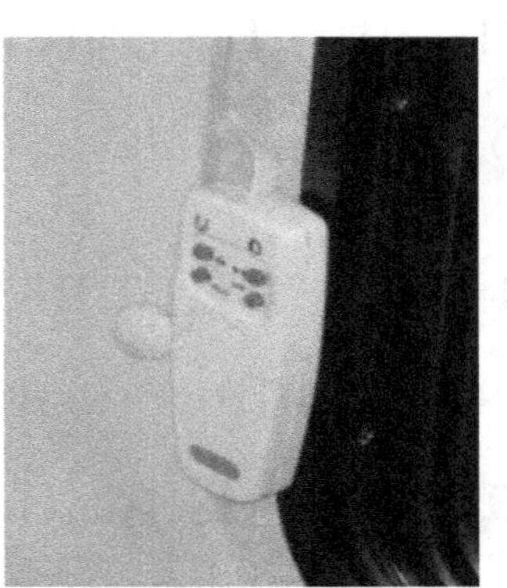

a

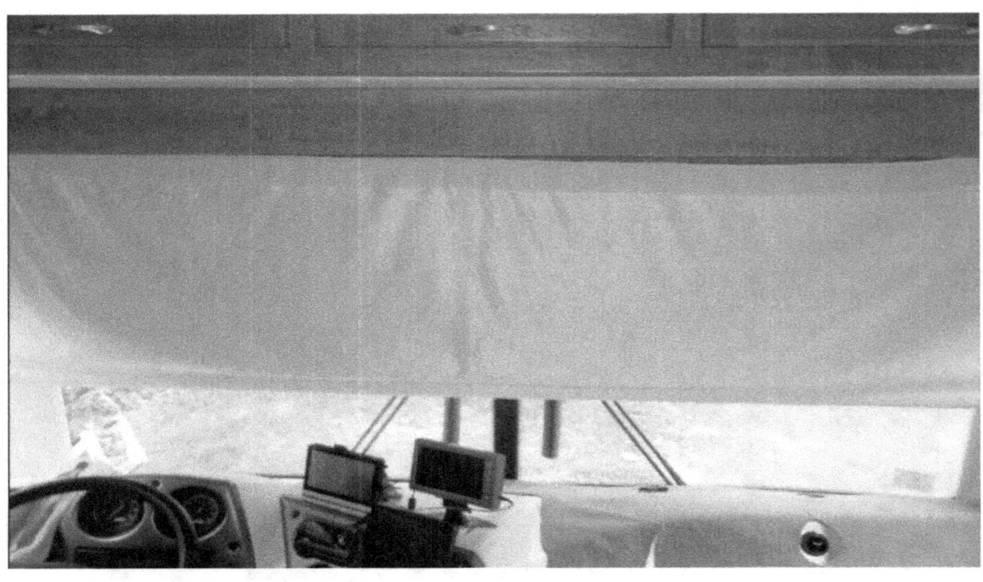

OUTSIDE FRONT WINDSHIELD SHADE

Again the best way to keep an RV cool is to keep the heat out. Even with my inside shade there was still a lot of heat getting in. It was getting trapped between the shade and the windshield. An outside shade was needed. I researched what was available on the market but did not like any of the mounting methods. At that time a ladder was needed for all of them and I wanted to be able to install my shade from the ground.

On with my thinking cap and I came up with a product that runs a bungee cord around two hooks I added to the top of my coach windshield. The cord can be routed with a pole from the ground. They then wrap around the mirror arm and attach back to the shade. This has worked great for years and my cost was only $50.00. All material was gotten off eBay.

WINDOW AWNINGS

I have said this twice before and I will say it again. The best way to keep an RV cool is to keep the heat out. Window awnings help tremendously to do this.

When installing window awnings I like to match the products the OEM has installed on the RV if any. In my case the OEM installed CAREFRE patio awning so I went to CAREFREE for the window awnings.

Decide which windows you want awnings for and measure the window width. CAREFREE says it is best to get an awning that extends beyond the window by four inches on each side. Decide how far out you want the awnings to drop and what material you would like them made from, place your order where by the seller will happily relieve you of your money. In my case it was $1080.00 for three awnings.

Installation was quite easy. The awnings come wiyh an awning rail, awning, and two arms each. The awning rail goes on first. Measure and mark a line three inches above the window. Put a strip of butyl putty on the awning rail and press it against the RV along the marked line. The putty will cause the rail to stick to the RV. Now with an electric drill and number 8 self tapping screws shoot a screw through each hole in the rail.

Slide on the awning, secure the arms and awning fabric, remove the cotter pin to release the awning spring, open the awning and measure for the hold down clip and install the clip. Done.

INSULATE AGAINST HEAT

Ok I shaded everything I could think of yet in 100 degree heat the air conditioners work all day and only cool the coach to 90 degrees. What is going on?

Reading posts on many forums I have learned that other RVers are insulating their air conditioner caps and vent caps. They line these with a product called Reflective Insulation. This is like foil bubble wrap.   To adhere it there is a special foil tape made by the same manufacturer. I insulated my two AC Covers and three MaxxAri Covers for $59.43.

I have a split bath in my coach with the water closet on the passenger side and shower on the driver's side. One hot July day when I walked from the front of the coach to the back I noticed a 20 degree heat gain in the shower area. The heat was coming in through the shower skylight.

While they give you more head room a lot of people like me see no other value for them.

As I continue to say the best way to keep the coach cool is keep the heat out. With that in mind I went up on the roof and painted out all but a six inch square opening on the skylight. The product I used was "KRYLON

FUSSION" paint specifically formulated for plastics.

Next to the inside of the coach I installed a shade over the skylight. On extremely hot days I pull this closed blocking off the remaining light and heat coming through the skylight.

With this and the other cooling efforts I finally began to have a positive effect on the heat issue in the coach.

The shade I installed was a new old stock item made by CAREFREE that is no longer available. If you like the idea I have found a comparable shade available now that costs about $15.00

"Lights Out Vent Shade" Opens to 14-1/8" x 19"

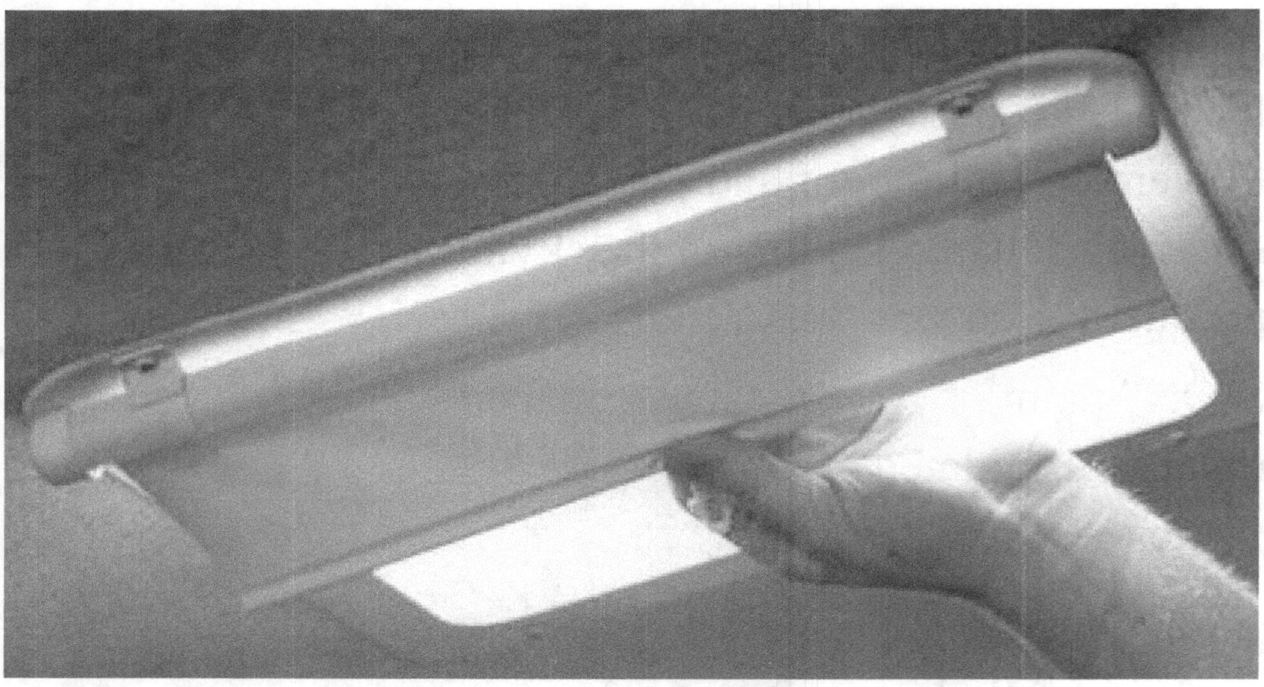

PAINT TOP OF AC & VENT COVERS WHITE

Still not satisfied with the temperatures in the coach on hot summer days I continued my research. One day while camping I had an opportunity to speak with a Dometic air conditioner engineer. He told me that coaches with white or light colored AC covers cooled 15 degrees lower than coaches with Black or dark color covers. I decided to paint out the tops of my AC covers and vent covers white. So back up to the roof I went with the white "KRYLON FUSSION". Guess what? He was right. This one fix has made the most dramatic difference in the ability of the air conditioners to keep up with the heat. By only painting the tops, from the ground they still look like you have the colored matching vents on the RV. This was a win win.

The KRYLON FUSSION sells for about $12.00 per can.

Who does not want more shade on those hot sunny days? I know I do but I am inherently lazy when I am out in the RV. I want the shade without asserting any effort. Shade Por came up with the solution, Vista-Shade. It is a shade screen for your awning. It comes in two sections. The upper section shown in the picture slips into the spare awing rail on your awning and remains there. Yes it can roll up with the awning, no muss no fuss. If you need additional shade there is a lower section that will zip on to the upper and can even be used as an awning stake down device. My vista for a 22 foot awing was $161.00

KEEP THE APPLIANCE DOOR CLOSED

OK you have made your first trip in the brand new rig loaded with residential appliances and you learned the doors of the refrigerator or dishwasher will not stay closed when the rig is in motion. This was painfully obvious to you as you cleaned up the condiment spills. Here is a product that will solve your problems. "The Multi-Purpose Appliance Lock" made by Safety 1st. You can find them at Walmart for just a few dollars.

For some the reason the builder of my coach choose not to vent the microwave range outside the coach but had it blow the air from the stove back in. Neither did they provide the vent filters for the microwave. In this situation one thing that happens is frequent false smoke alarms during meal preparation. An outside vent was necessary but which one. I finally found a vent I liked here http://www.rvstuff.com for $22.95. The vent comes in white or black. I chose black.

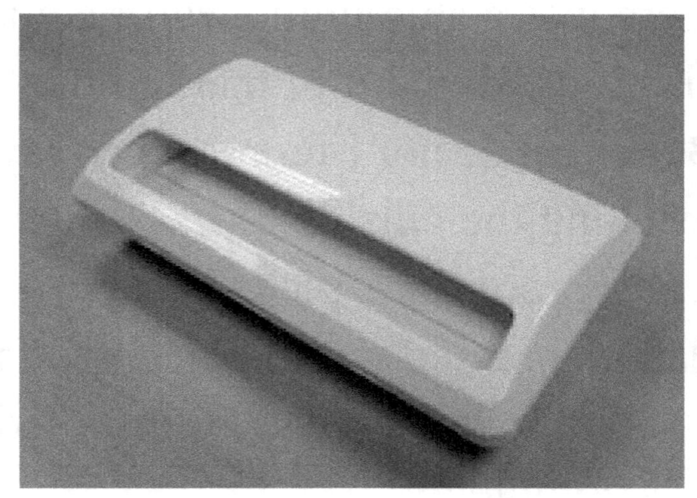

Next I consulted the microwave manual to learn how the microwave was mounted and how to convert it to an external fan. From this I determined I had to remove the bottom of the cabinet above the microwave

to get to the mounting screws. This was done by carefully prying with a putty knife.   I placed a stool and pillow on the stove as I loosened and removed the microwave to reveal the wall behind it.

Not knowing what was in the wall I decided to remove one wall layer at a time using my multi-tool. My thoughts were if there was a stud in the wall I could leave it in place and let the air blow around it. I marked the location to cut and began. Believe it or not I found seven layers of material before reaching the outside. I lined the hole with steel tape to create a water proof duct, placed a strip of butyl tape around the outside flange, pressed it into place and fastened with 3/4 inch number 6 self tapping screws. Reinstalled the microwave and the job was complete.

How many of you know how well your RV refrigerator is cooling? I would imagine not too many. Even if you have a thermometer in the refrigerator by the time you open the door and retrieve it, it will have warmed by some amount thus providing an inaccurate reading.

I read about this modification on an RV forum, liked it and have done it about ½ dozen times. Mount 12 volt digital temperature monitors in the control panel of the refrigerator. These are readily available on eBay. Just be sure to look for 12 volt dc operation. Cost should not be more than $4.00 each. At that price I got an extra in the event of a failure I would have the exact same model as a replacement. The thermal couple wire is run down the hinge side of the frame. I held mine in place with a dab of GE silicone, then ran the temperature bulbs, one into the freezer compartment and the other into the refrigerator, and secured them with tie wraps to a shelf.

The front panel of the refrigerator is removed by depressing two clips, one on each side. You have to look to see them. Using a multi meter you can test connections on the refrigerator control board to find 12 volt power that is on when refrigerator is on and off when refrigerator is off.

For those of you that are not handy, this product allows you to monitor the temperature in both your refrigerator and freezer. Installation is a breeze. You just need to replace the batteries every year. Cost is about $25.00 and you can find it here.here

https://www.amazon.com/AcuRite-00986A2-Refrigerator-Wireless-Thermometer/dp/B004QJVU78/ref=sr_1_3?ie=UTF8&qid=1509236957&sr=8-3&keywords=Refrigerator+Digital+Thermometer

The product name is "AcuRite 00986A2 Refrigerator Freezer Wireless Digital Thermometer"

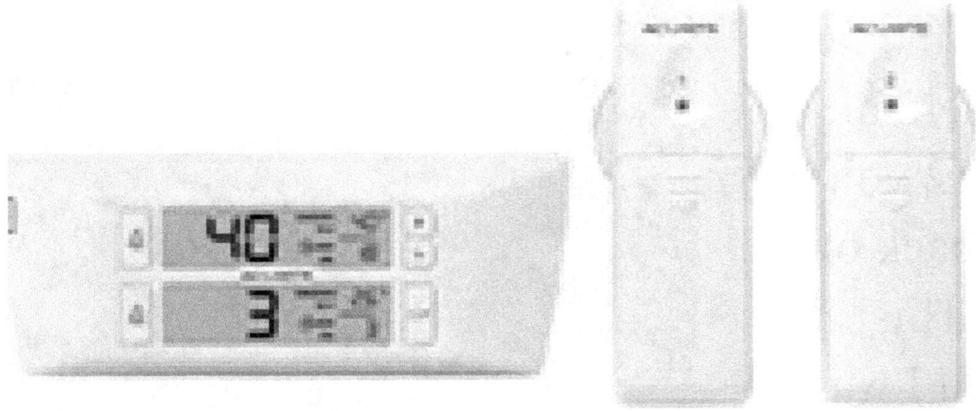

IMPROVING REFRIGERATOR COOLING

I have often read that an RV refrigerator will run more efficiently if you can exhaust the heat from the back of the unit. There are many kits on the market that claim to do this for you at the cost of $65.00 for a basic kit to over $100.00 that runs the fan off a solar cell. You can however make one of these kits yourself for a few dollars.

I did this by purchasing a thermal switch on eBay that closes at 45 degrees C. The switch was $4.00 for two. I then grabbed two, three inch, 12 volt computer fans. These I mounted in the vent of my refrigerator to push the air up and out the stack. I wired the fans through the thermal switch to the 12 volt supply at the back of the refrigerator.   This worked so well I was able to get the same cooling and turn my

refrigerator settings down by half.

Attached are pictures of the install.

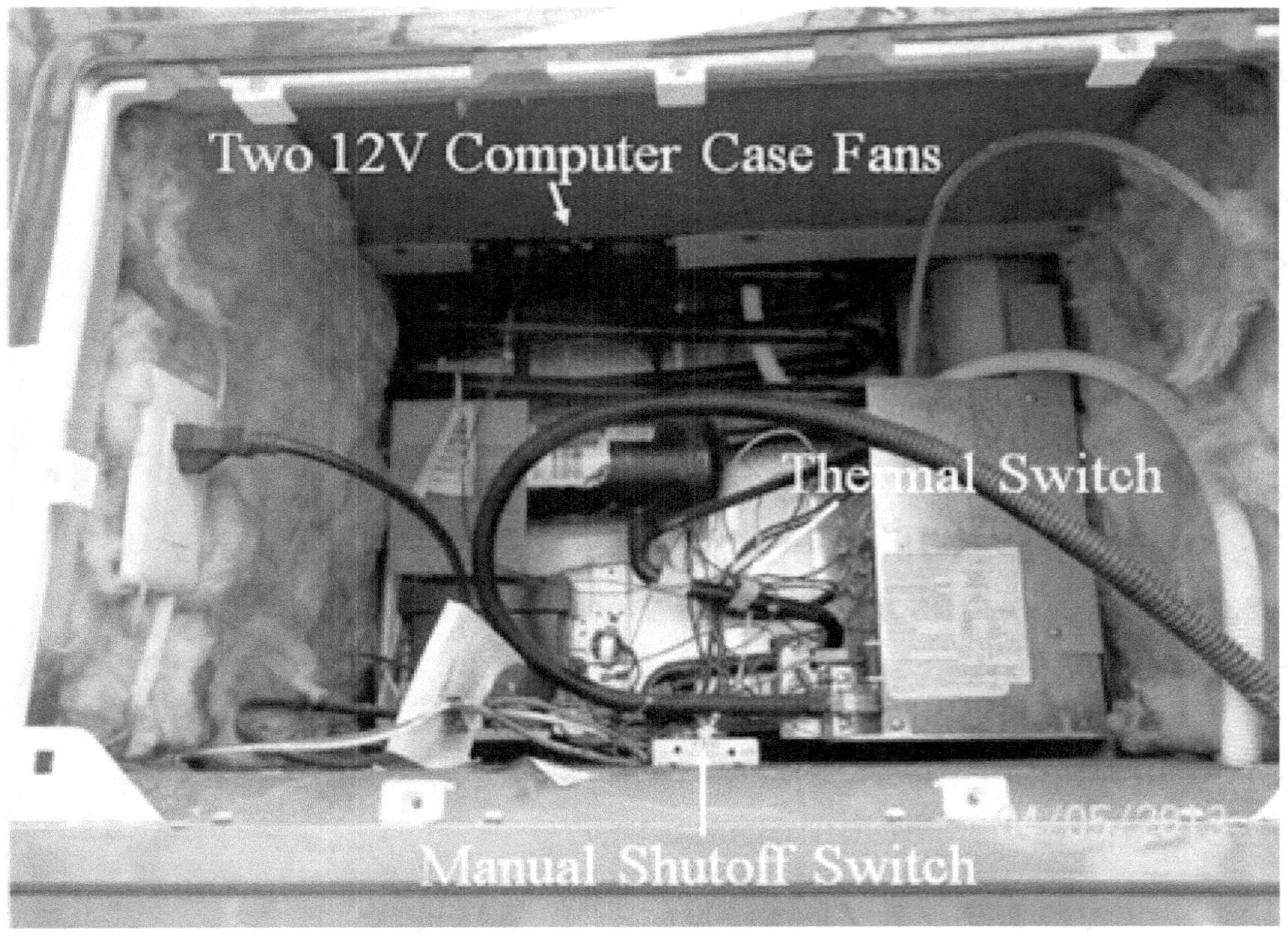

IMPROVING REFRIGERATOR COOLING REV II

If you read the previous section you know the reason for this modification and how well it works. So why a REV II? The scrap fans I grabbed moved a lot of air but at a cost, noise. Sitting in the coach at night I could hear this high pitched scream that drove me nuts. I guess it does not pay to cheep out all the time. I went out to the net and found two larger but quieter 60db fans. Because they were larger they did not fit where I had the original fans. My solution was to fabricate a directional duct for one and have the other blow directly onto the exposed condenser. The thermal switch and wiring remained the same.

Below are the pictures of the duct and install. The duct is cardboard wrapped in aluminum tape.

TV ANTENNA UPGRADE

In the early 2000s the world transitioned from analog to digital TV. Unfortunately not everyone in the RV industry was quite as quick to upgrade. My 2008 motorhome had digital TVs but an old analog antenna. An easy and cost effectively solution is to replace just the head of the antenna but keep the mast. The JACK antenna has an option for just this. Easy to install it only takes 15 minutes and you are done. Cost is just under $50.00.

ENERGY MANAGEMENT SYSTEM

With the quality of power in many campgrounds and the investment RV owners have in their electronics at some time everyone should consider getting an EMS (Energy Management System). I went with a system from Progressive Industries, the EMS50. At the time of my purchase they were $350.00 and I believed they are still in that price range. When I purchased Progressive industries offered a life time warranty. If the unit failed you could unplug the faulty circuit card and easily plug in a replacement. To install all I did was cut my main power cord and placed the EMS50 between the cut ends. The instructions were very clear.

I have had mine installed for nine years. In that time it has never failed. On several occasions while attending large RV rallies there have been power problems that have caused serious faults in neighbors' RVs but my EMS50 just shuts down power when it sees a fault saving my coach from damage.

The EMS50 fault check with codes are:

E-0 Normal Conditions
E-1 Reverse Polarity Condition (hot and neutral wires reversed)
E-2 Open Ground
E-3 Line 1 Voltage High (Line voltage above 132 volts)
E-4 Line 1 Voltage Low (Line voltage below 104 volts)
E-5 Line 2 Voltage High (Line voltage above 132 volts)
E-6 Line 2 Voltage Low (Line voltage below 104 volts)
E-7 Line Frequency High (Line frequency above 69 cycles per second)
E-8 Line Frequency Low (Line frequency below 51 cycles per second)
E-9 Data Link Down
E-10 Replace Surge Protector Module

In addition to the 50 amp power management system I have, the company also makes a 30 amp system and portable systems.

To follow is a block diagram of an install.

POWER CORD REEL

Have you ever tried to coil up a 50 amp electric cord in April or October up in the Northeast? It is a pain. I loved to go out on the weekends but hated getting ready to come home due to the power cord issue. I looked at power cord reels but just could not bring myself to spend $650.00, the typical price. Then one spring they went on sale, down $200.00 to $450.00. Still a high price but I went for it and believe me this has been one of the best modifications I have made. It is even worth the non sale price. I installed mine with a remote but have never used it.

To find one just search the internet for RV Power cord reel.

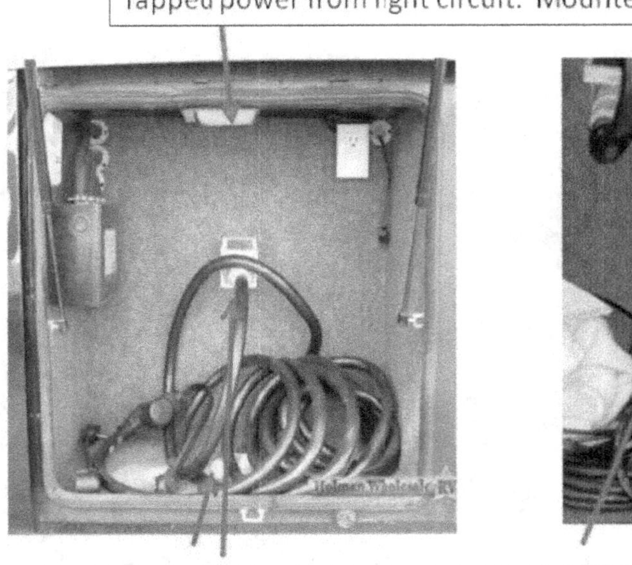

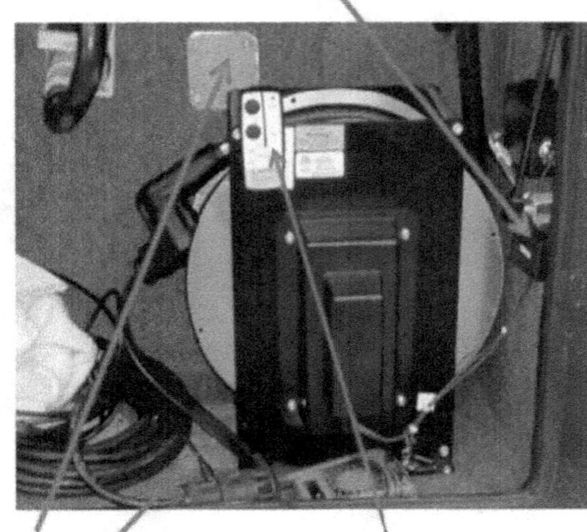

Needed to move original power input and output. You can see cap I placed over the old holes. Reused original parts.

Added a remote control From winch. Found I never Use it.

POWER TRANSFORMER

As time moves on there are always new toys to be had. Here in the Northeast there are a lot of old campgrounds with shoddy power. The Progressive industry EMS50 protects the coach but wouldn't it be nice if you could clean up and boost the power just like the power company does with the power transformer up on the power pole. Well now you can with a HUGHES Autoformer.

Per their instructions you cannot hardwire the autoformer to your RV. Rather they sell a cord set that allows it to be plugged in. They also request that the cabinet the autoformer is installed in be vented.

To follow is my install. Total cost $555.00.

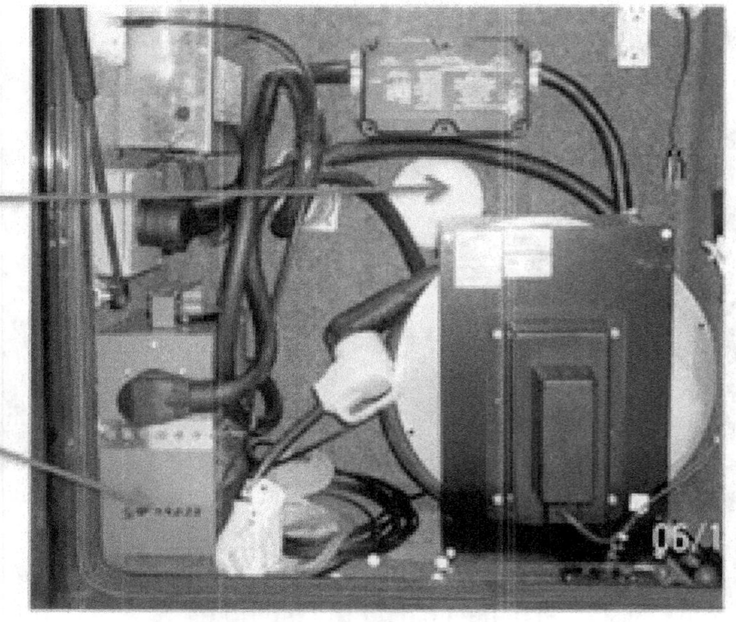

Schematic wise this is what the install looks like

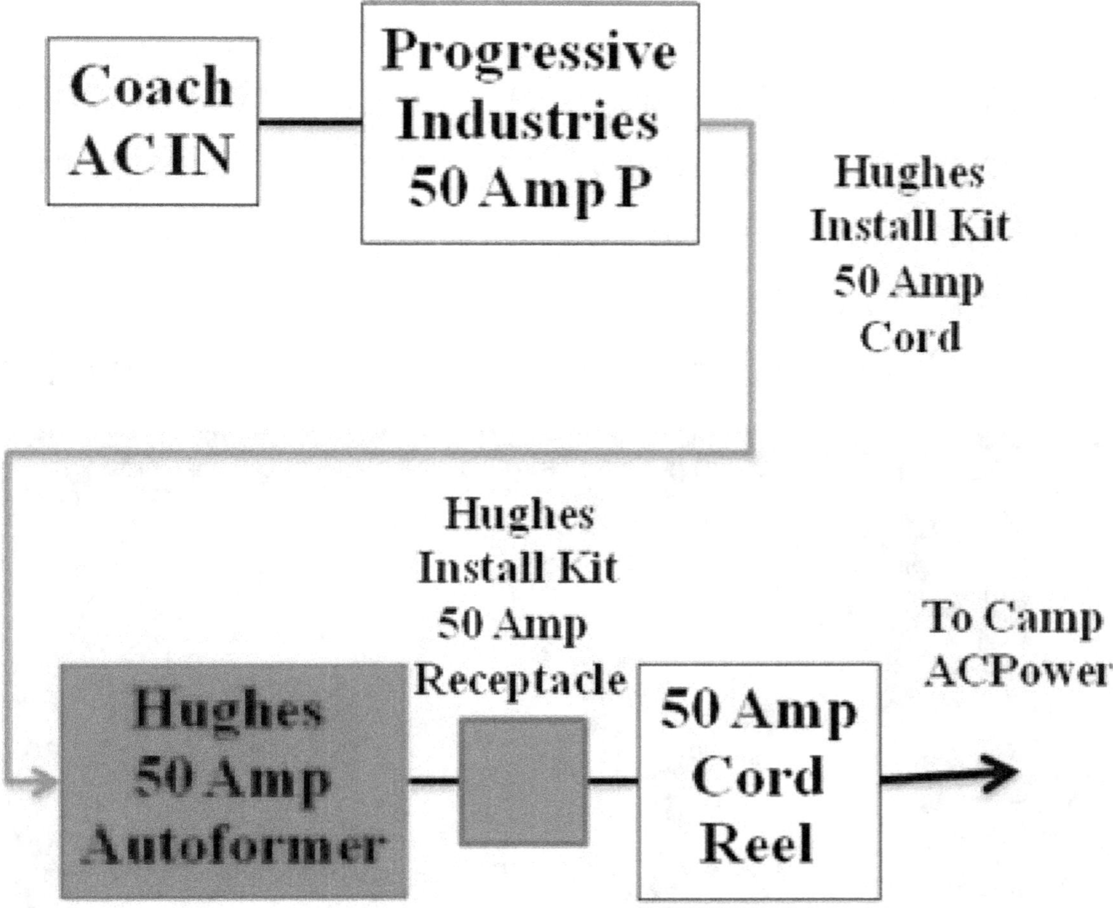

Hughes also makes autoformers for 30 amp service.

DOG BONE ORGANIZER

No not the kind you feed the dog but your electrical dog bones. I have three and they were always lying at the bottom of my electrical cabinet blocking the cord exit hole. One day while walking through Wal-Mart I saw a broom holder and thought that is just what I need. For $8.00 I had a dog bone organizer.

BATTERY VOLT METER

I have always wanted a permanently installed volt meter so I could check my motorhomes batteries without having to take them out. The solution required a meter that could be turned on and off so it would not constantly drain the batteries and had to have its own power supply because you will want to check the batteries when low and bad batteries could affect your readings. Then it came to me, one of those inexpensive Harbor Freight multi meters wired into the battery bank met all the criteria.

With my setup I can check the chassis battery bank, coach battery bank and each individual 6 volt coach battery.

This is the install

I built the custom wire run,

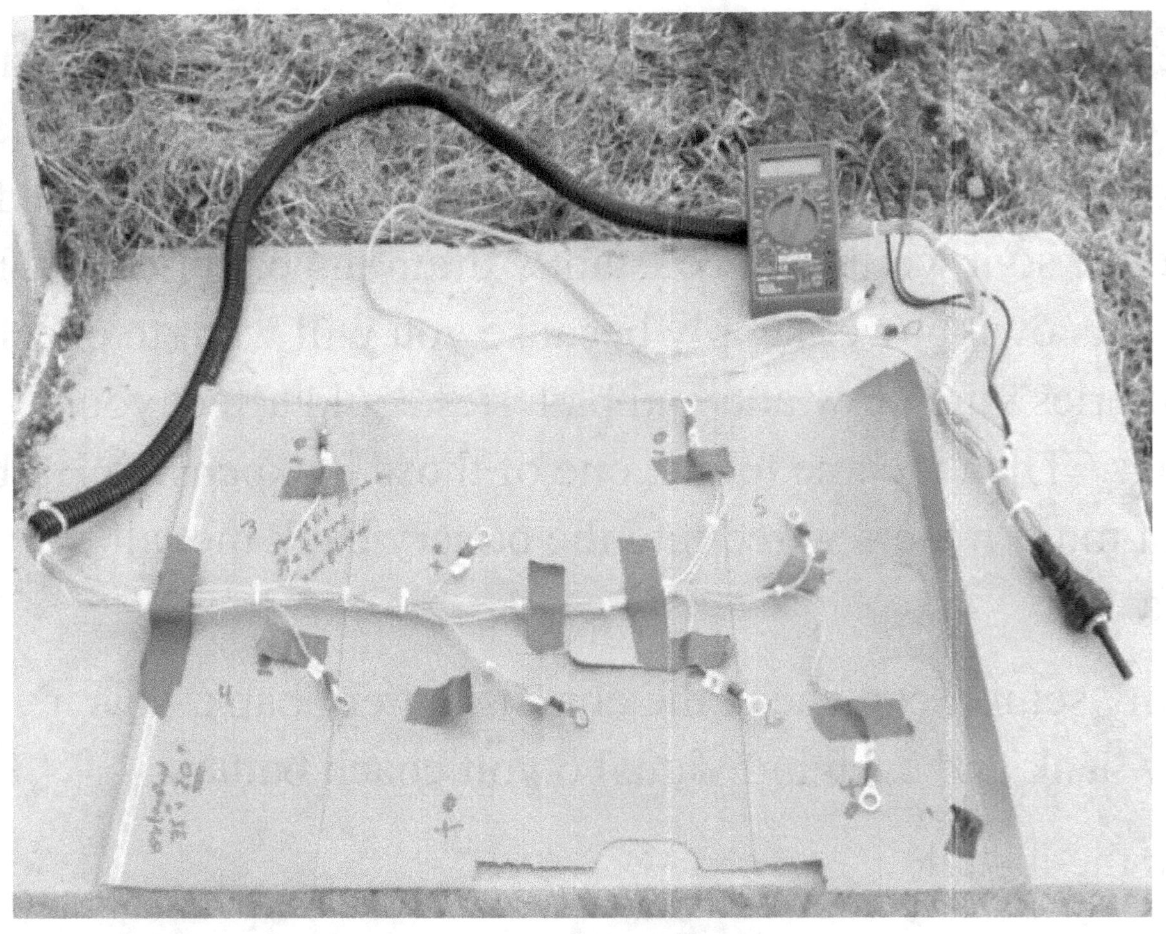

EXTERIOR POWER OUTLET

Every RV I have ever owned has had an outside power outlet except this motorhome. Sit under the awning and want to play the radio, too bad. Want to plug in the electric skillet and cook breakfast on the picnic table, too bad. A modification was needed. For $20 I installed a power box and outlet. I ran the wiring up into the kitchen and tapped into one of the ground fault circuits. Love it.

Don't be afraid to cut holes in your RV. Just plan out the project and go slow. Remember measure twice and cut once. It will work out. If it does not that is what they make those US map stickers for.

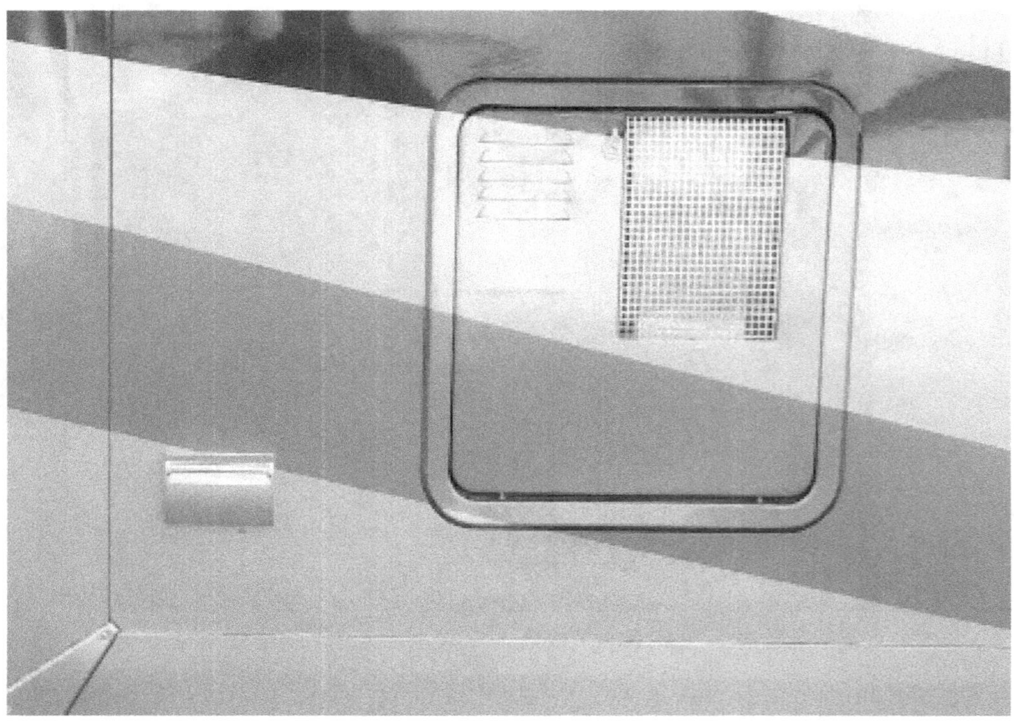

INTERIOR POWER OUTLET

There are never enough power outlets in the typical RV. Especially at the table where one often likes to use their laptop or charge their cell phones and other USB type devices. An elegant solution to this problem is to install additional outlets as depicted in the picture. You get both USB outlets as well as standard 120 volt outlets. When not in use the outlets hide in the table top. The outlets can be found at this internet address.

Search on Amazon for "BINGONE Hide-power Pull-up Station Desktop, Three Outlets, Plastic & Aluminum, US Version, Black (black top, USB up)"

This is what the install looks like.

BATTERY TENDER

When fall approaches you should be thinking of what to do to get the RV ready for winter. What will you do about the RV battery? I have used two of these for the past several years to keep my batteries fresh through the winter months. I have one connected to my bank of four coach 6 volt batteries and one connected to my bank of two 12 volt chassis batteries and they work great. All I do is be sure to top off the battery water and plug them in. I am set for the winter. A plus with these is you can keep them connected through the summer months when you are using the RV and they do not interfere with your on board battery charger. They are a no muss no fuss solution. Harbor Freight normally has them on sale in the fall for $19.98. This is a great price for a battery charger/tender.

You can find them here https://www.harborfreight.com/15-amp-three-stage-onboard-battery-charger-maintainer-99857.html

1.5 Amp Three Stage Onboard 12V Battery

Cen-Tech® - Item#99857

I researched this project for over a year reading hundreds of white papers and talking to even more people. One thing that became apparent back in 2016 was there are a lot of companies installing solar on RVs but none are documenting the why or the how. Starting from nothing and after my year long research I felt ready to begin specifying my system.

I decided I wanted monocrystalline type solar panels, an MPPT charge controller and I needed a minimum of 175 watts of solar to sustain my energy needs. Energy use is going to be different for everyone. I took into consideration that my wife and I are very thrifty with our RV energy. I have a generator if I need to run the coffee pot, microwave, or air conditioner. All I need the solar for is to replenish the batteries after a day's use of the ceiling fan, lights, cell phone charger, power used by the gas refrigerator controller, propane detector, and TV. I also wanted a system that could be expanded if required.

Through my research I had decided I would purchase the bulk of the needed material from Renogy Solar. Armed with my requirements I began to design my system. As I did the costs kept climbing and climbing until I realized it would be cheaper to just purchase one of their 200 watt package deals. The problem with the 200 watt package was it was maxed out and could not be expanded so I settled on the Renogy 300 watt MPPT package. The timing was near Christmas 2015 and Renogy had their packages on sale. By waiting until Cyber Monday I was able to secure an additional 15% discount over the sale price. After purchasing switches and mounting hardware my total installation cost was $733.51.   Really not bad.

Here is a breakdown of the material:

KIT-PREMIUM300D-MT Renogy 300 Watt 12 Volt Monocrystalline Solar Premium Kit	$623.23
15 FEET SunGen Solar Panel Extension Cable Wire (15 Ft.) with MC4 Connectors	$9.99
6 FEET UL Solar Panel Extension Cable Wire (6 ft) with MC4 Connectors	$11.99
Marine Knob Battery Master Isolator Cut Off Power Kill Switch Control 12/24V	$18.08
Winegard CE-2000 RV Roof Cable Entry Plate	$8.56
12V-24V DC Auto Car Bike Stereo Audio Circuit Breaker Reset Fuse Inverter GBNG 40 Amp	$8.25
100X Nylon Cable Zip Tie Mounts 20*20mm Self-Adhesive Wall Holder Mount Clip DIY	$2.98
Solar panel mounting hardware from www.mcmaster.com	$50.43
Total	$733.51

We dry camp about two weeks each year. I have used this system several times and after an evening with lights and TV going and two ceiling fans running all night, my batteries have been fully charged no later than 10:00 each morning.

Solar panel install.

There are a lot of discussions on this topic. Two popular areas are should they be on tilted brackets and do you to fasten them.

First the bracket.

I decided since I had excess capacity in my design I would install the panels flat on the roof of the RV. I had no interest climbing up on there to tilt the panels.

Now the fastening question.

You will not believe how many people will not drill holes in their roof but look to tape, Velcro, or only dicor to attach their panels.   I just want to say I do not want to follow these people down the road. I have seen panels blow off and a flying panel is not easy to dodge. The solar panel must be anchored and anchored well. Renogy recommends the use of well nuts and their Z brackets and well nuts to anchor their panels.

Well nuts can hold almost anything to the thinnest of materials. Well nuts can be found in the specialty section of the large box stores.

Below is a graphic showing how they work.

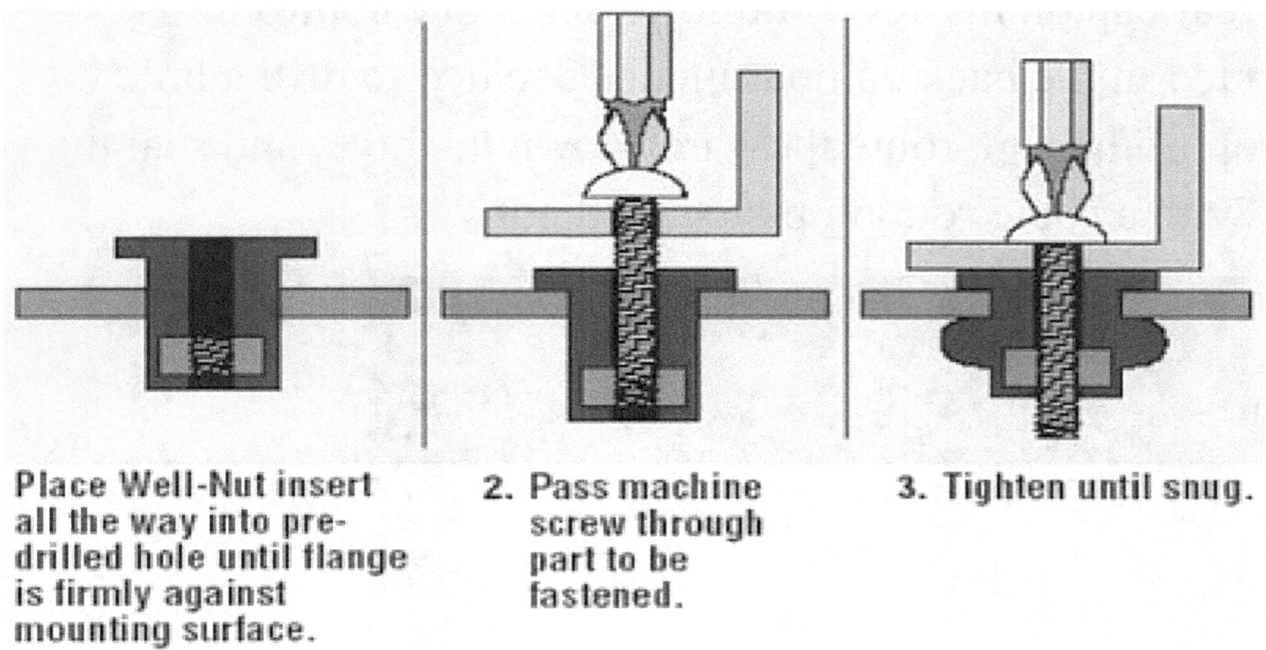

Upon securing the panels I followed up with an ample application of dicor around the brackets and screw heads to prevent leaks. My panels have been installed for two years. So far no leaks and solid as a rock.

To get the maximum from my solar panels I wired them in series. The panel wiring is held down to the RV roof with dabs of dicor.

Now the question of routing the wires from the roof to the RV basement and to the solar controller. There are several ways to accomplish this. Some people will drill holes in their gray water tank vent stack, route the wires down the stack, then seal the holes. This is a great idea.

Others route down the refrigerator stack, another great idea.

The rear cap on my RV is hollow. Since the controller is mounted in the back compartment I decided to drill a hole in the top of the cap, route the wires down the hole, and seal the hole with a cable routing plate and dicor.

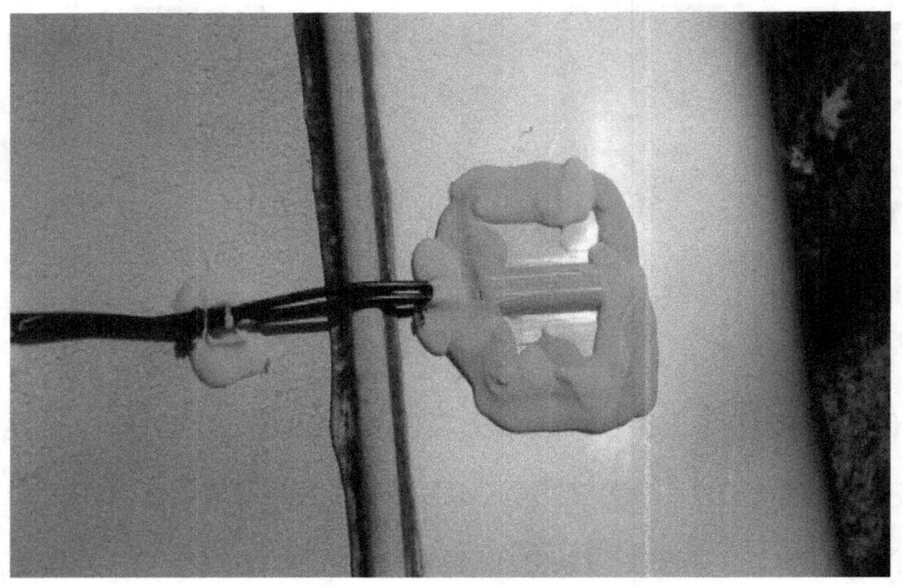

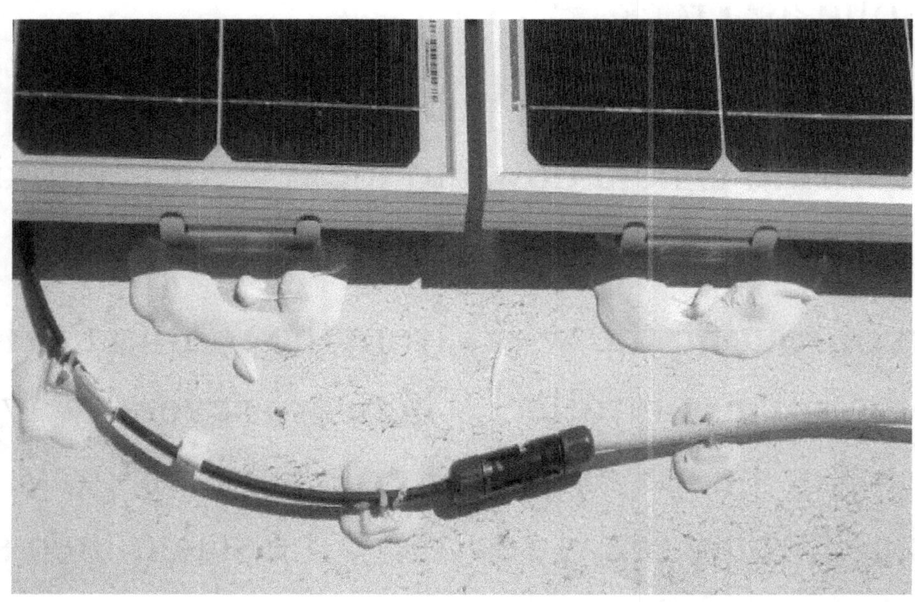

Everything you read says to install the solar controller near the batteries so as to minimize cable length. On my RV the inverter/converter is in the back basement cabinet and the batteries are in the cabinet right next to it, perfect. I mounted the solar controller using two wooden slats so it would be away from the wall allowing air flow and cooling. I have an on off switch and fuse between the controller and solar panels. I have another resettable fuse between the controller and the batteries.

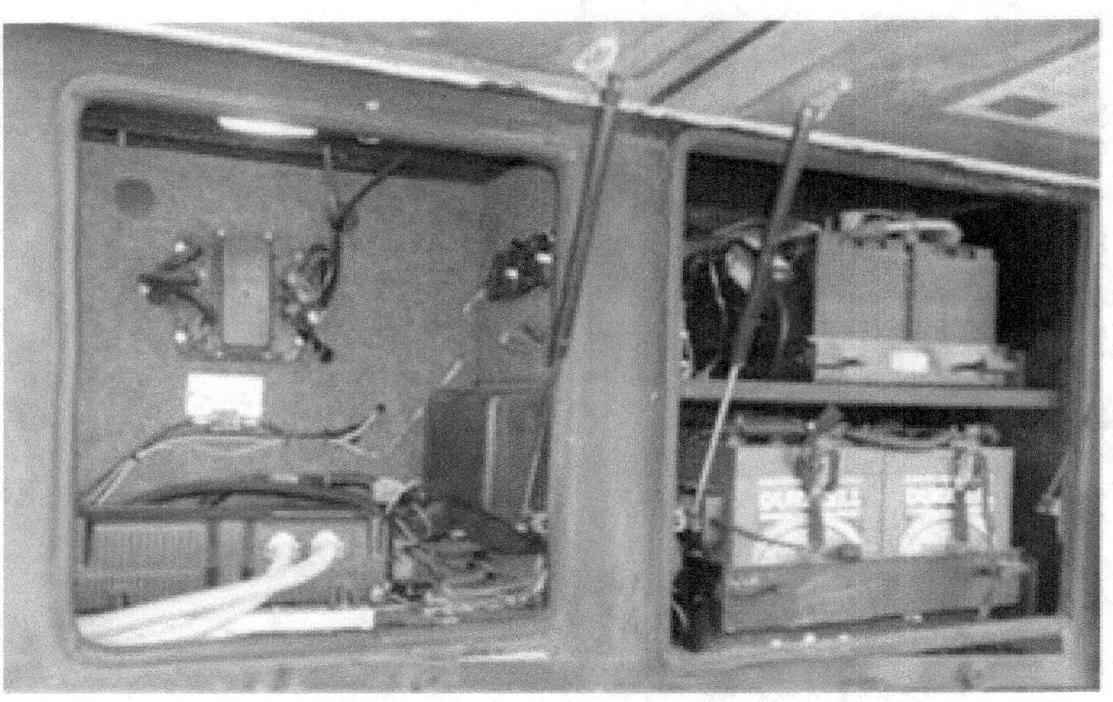

Photo Showing Location of Electronics Bay With Respect to Battery Bay

Renogy MPPT 40
Amp Controller
Photo Panel
Disconnect Switch
04/14/2016

40 Amp Fuse and Battery
Disconnect Switch
04/14/2016

One topic that I could find absolutely no information on was if you need any special considerations when installing a solar controller on an RV that has an inverter/converter. Would the two fight each other when charging the batteries? The answer is no. If the Renogy solar contoller sees elevated voltage on the battery bank from another charger it will shut down.

The MTTP controller I selected is capable of talking to a remote information and control panel. The last portion of my install was to route a CAT4 cable into the cabin of the RV and connect this control panel.

Some web sites that I found useful in my information search are listed below

http://gpelectric.com/products/solar-flex-kits-modules

https://www.windynation.com/

https://www.renogy.com/

http://samlexsolar.com/

Most motorhomes have one or at most two 12 volt convince outlets in the dash. With all the toys that are now available such as GPS, rear cameras systems, satellite radios, tire pressure monitor systems and dash cameras there are just not enough outlets. Additionally the outlets that are available are either tied to the key or hot all the time. What if you want the flexibility to have both? The solution I had is to add outlets either under the dash or in the dash itself. In the picture below I have added additional outlets to the dash of my motorhome mounted under an access panel. In my case I added four additional outlets. You can get 12 volt outlet USB charge port combinations providing even more capability and flexibility.

My motorhome has a feature that I can run the dash radio with the key on or key off. This is accomplished with a manufacture installed dash switch that connects the radio either to the chassis batteries through the key on position or directly to the coach batteries. I decided to tie my added 12 volt outlets into the radio power line so they would have this capability to. The line was easy to find as all the wires coming out of the back of my radio have been well labeled. If yours are not just check the radio manual.

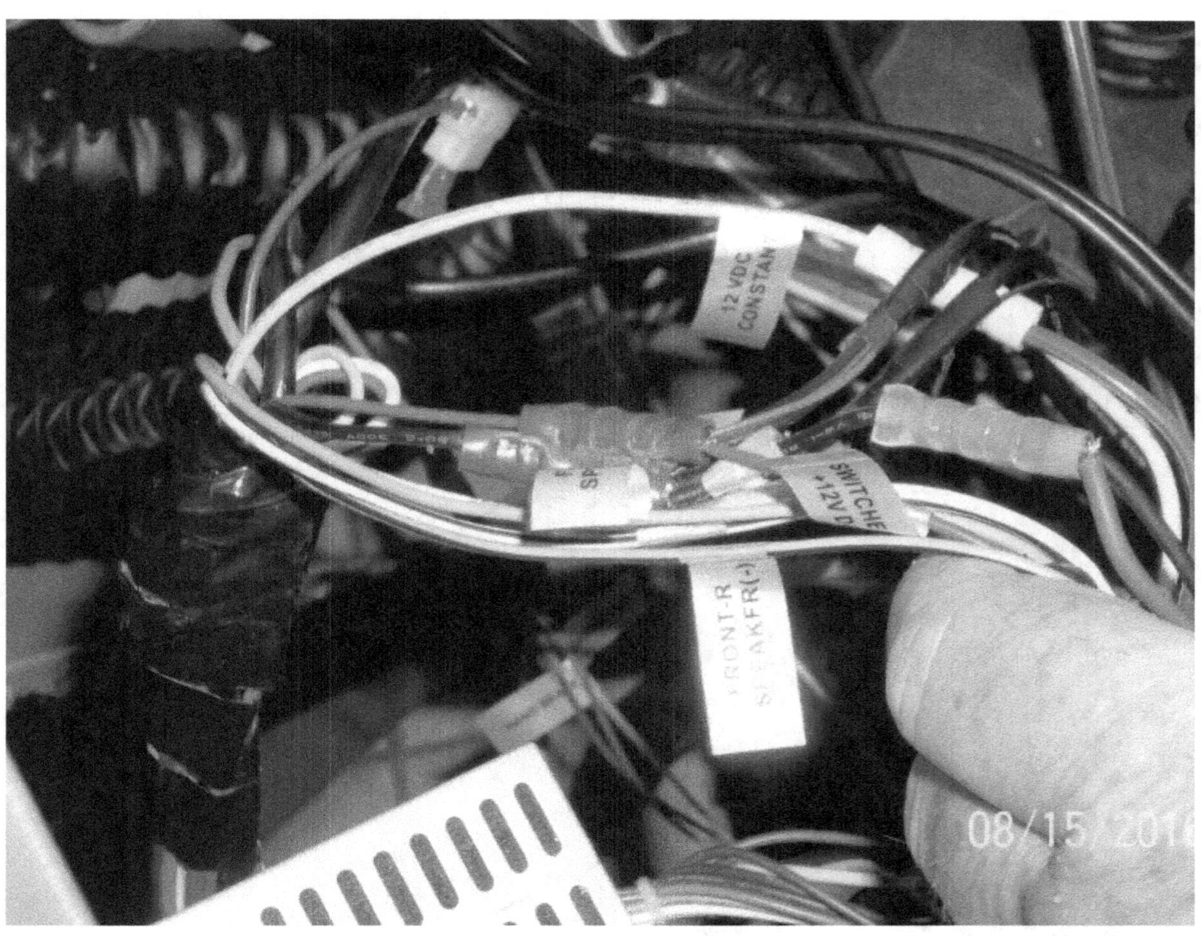

All the toys we talked about in the previous section such as GPS, rear cameras systems, satellite radios, tire pressure monitor systems, dash cameras normally have suction cup mounts to hold them in place. These were designed for use on glass such as the windshield however a motorhome windshield is normally three feet to four feet in front of the driver. You can't see them well nor can you reach then if you need to interact with them.   The solution I have is to mount a piece of plexi-glass to the dash. This provides a location to mount all the toys. An additional feature you may want to implement is to place a cable router plug in the dash as shown. This allows the cables for the toys to be neatly routed behind and into the dash rather than having them draped down over the front of the dash.

My motorhome came with power sun shades for the windshield but not the side windows. As you encounter different driving conditions sun from the side can be a problem. I was looking for a solution when I ran into Shade-Pro at a trade show. They were selling CAREFREE new old stock shades with control switches. While I needed a four foot shade (they were sold out) they did have two foot shades. Normally these CARFREE Shades sell for $399.00 each. Shade-Pro were selling them for $25.00 each. How could I say no?

I mounted two shades on the driver side window running the control wire down the A pillar. Picked up power from the 12 volt socket on the dash and installed the switches in a convent location to be reached when driving. Here are the results.

If you have read my book, thank you. It took me sixty year to get this far. I hope that it did not take you quite that long to read it.

James Edward Clicquennoi

Traveling with my parents when younger and then my own family I have been RVing for over 60 years. Between my father and I we have owned 9 different types of RVs from simple pop ups, travel trailers, and finally a diesel pusher motorhome. In that time we have never taken our RV to anyone else for repairs or to add modifications. In my later life not only have I done all my own repairs but I have helped friends and collogues in my travel clubs do theirs. In the past 15 years I began enhancing my RVs as well as friends with those options not installed by the manufacturer. This book describes with pictures and illustrations the close to 100 modifications I have performed. Some are simple and inexpensive while others are very complex. This book is intended to give you, the reader the information necessary to install these options on your own RV.

www.ingramcontent.com/pod-product-compliance
Lightning Source LLC
Chambersburg PA
CBHW081719250726
48657CB00010B/3054